Top 30 low startup cost business

NATHAN M. FLOWERS

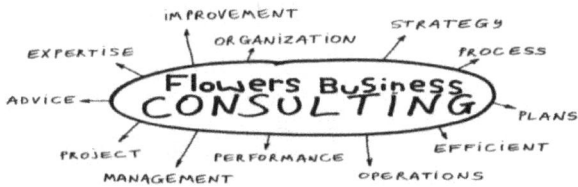

Copyright © 2016 Nathan M. Flowers

All rights reserved. No part of this book may be reproduced or transmitted in any form by and means, electronic or mechanical, including photocopying and recording, or by any information storage and retrieval system, except as may be expressly permitted by the 1976 Copyright Act or by the publisher.

Contents

Introduction

Chapters:

1. Sales consultant

2. Freelance bookkeeper

3. Cleaning service

4. Personal chef

5. Personal trainer

6. Concierge Service

7. Home bakery

8. Business coach

9. Child care service

10. Computer service and repair

11. Debt Collection agency

12. Dog walking

13. Home Sewing Business

14. Craft Business

15. Information Consultant

16. Lawn Moving

17. Legal Transcription

18. Mobile Pet Grooming

19. Medical Transcription

20. Online Retailer

21. Photography

22. Senior Care Services

23. Tour guide operator

24. Translation service

25. Tutoring

26. Virtual Assistant

27. Web Designing

28. Wedding Planner

29. Yoga Instructor

30. Social media assistant

1. <u>Sales Consultant – Direct sales arena</u>

What is it all about?

It is a billion dollar retail channel in the United States and one of the oldest forms of distribution of products. It is widely used by some of the world's most recognizable brands to market products and services to consumers. Direct selling involves a sales force of millions of committed independent entrepreneurs or sales consultants. These independent consultants are affiliated with a direct selling company and receive commissions on sales. It is mainly done via home shopping parties, presentations or by catalog sales.

Advantages of direct sales.

- Flexible hours: You have to work, but you get to choose when to do it. You can work when you want and from where you want.

- Low Startup Investment: The cost of getting started is very minimal. Thus provides an advantage of recouping back your money and begin being profitable faster.

- Brand name products: Having products that people are instantly familiar with and consume is huge when you are making a commission. It is fun being a part of a company that has the "it" products.

- Amazing training: Many of the Direct Sales organizations have top-rated training programs and receiving the proper training is advantageous for your success and for building the business.

- Everyone can do it: Flexible income opportunity to men and women, across all ages, level of experience and social origins.

- Social contact and personal recognition: Friendships with customers, business partners, Up-line and Down- line personal, building a customer network base is a great way to get to know many people from many walks of life. It is self-rewarding to help customers by providing excellent products at a fair price.

- Be your own boss and work from anywhere: Freedom on your hands to do what you want and how much you want to earn on your schedule from where you want.

- Unlimited earning potential: It all depends on the individual capacity. Can go from making extra money to a full-fledged business structure. As Bonnie Cribbs, in his blog on "Helping home based business owners grow by teaching; Social media and online marketing strategies" compares sales consultants of Direct sales to Beach Money CEO because it's like that people earn extra money for their beach vacations. Or, if they want, to build their dream house on the beach. The business model of MLM and Direct Sales is such that the earning potential truly is unlimited.

Ideal for you: If?

If you are a self-starter, confident, ability to communicate with people one on one and are truly excited and passionate about the products you are selling, a career in direct sales is ideal for you.

Though it is not as time demanding as some other business ventures, the success of the business depends upon building the customer base. The first prospects and buyers will be family, friends and /or coworkers.

Strategies to Success:

1.	Identify a product: Choose a product or service that you believe in and love.
2.	Choose the company: Identify a company that offers the type of product of your interest.
3.	Contact consumer watchdogs: Research and gather information about the company. Its background, history of complaints etc. Talking to former or current direct sales reps to get their experience.
4.	Industry Literate: Read all company literature and do it thoroughly. Also go through the company's product brochure, marketing materials, distributor details. Get knowledge on the company's financial statements at least for the past 5 years.
5.	Question to ask: should be Plenty and gather information about company's policy and procedures
6.	Size up costs: Make sure entry cost is modest. Beware of service fee and privilege joining fee.
7.	Return Policy Review: Know about company's buy back policy on unsold goods. Be cautious on buying large inventories especially at discounted price. A

good policy would be where the company buys back at least 90% of unsold, good conditioned inventory.

8. Compensation: Understand compensation plan, make sure there are no hidden clauses.

Examples:

The top 10 most brand value items listed on Direct sales with billions of sales are Amway, Avon, Heralife, Vorwerk, Mary Kay, Natura, Nu Skin, Tupperware, Belcorp and Oriflame.

Start up costs for some companies is as listed: Avon costs just $5 to register, Amway costs around $67, Pampered Chef is $80; both Tupperware and Mary Kay cost $100 to start with each company.

Possible disadvantages:

Quota; a necessary evil: Most sales companies have a quota to be met in order to retain active status as a consultant.

Independent contractor status: Important to keep track of income and business expenses and also to file taxes quarterly.

Competition: Comes from various angles; Local consultant competition, in-store products with low price tags.

Rejection: Rejection rates are higher than acceptance. Training and learning to market products help to change this rejection to acceptance ratio.

2. <u>Freelance Bookkeeping</u>

What is it all about?
Bookkeeping is all about recording, storing and retrieving of financial transactions.
The most common financial transactions and tasks involved in bookkeeping are:
1. Bills: Keep track of bills for goods sold or service provided.
2. Receipts: Recording receipts from customers
3. Invoices: verifying and recording invoices from suppliers
4. Payment: Calculation pay amounts to suppliers

5.   Pay Processing: Keep track of pay process for employees

6.   Monitor: Keep track of individual accounts receivable (money that is due to the company as it already has provided a good sales/service)

7.   Recording: Keep track of depreciation and other adjusting entries

8.   Reports: Provide financial reports

The successful operation of a company is highly dependent on accurate bookkeeping and payroll services. Freelance bookkeepers come into play for those companies, who cannot afford to hire permanent staff and other small companies, whose financial requirements are small, that they do not require permanent staff.

Advantages of Freelance Bookkeeping;

There is no particular schedule to adhere and can plan your own work schedule according to your convenience.

Be your own boss. You are free to take as many breaks as you want and when you want without someone looking over your shoulder.

No office space required, can work anywhere, as long as you have a computer, internet connection and access to the clients bookkeeping systems.

One of the positive benefits of freelance bookkeeping is that you will have an unlimited paycheck. The only limit to your earning is you- might have too much on your plate if you keep adding new clients more than you have time to work.

Many companies outsource bookkeeping on a regular basis to cut overhead expenses, so you are never out of work.

Ideal for you; If?
If you are a person who is detail oriented, a lover of numbers and pathologically honest, then bookkeeping is a perfect match for you. If you have a knowledge of debits and credits and a basic understanding of financial accounting, which includes the balance sheet and income statement, then freelance bookkeeping is defiantly a choice for you.

Strategies to Success:

1. First step of hurdle towards success: Finding your first freelance job:

The key to succeeding is to lower your fee from normal rate and consider taking any fee you get to win your first job. For example, say that your rate is $30/hour, and you get an offer for $15/hour. Then take the deal, but a smart way to succeed is to build in a raise after a month of or so: "I'll do it for $15/hour, but if you like my work, I want $20 (or $25 or $30) an hour after 30 days." Side effect; many prospects will accept your offer, planning to drop you after 30 days. But if you do quality work—correct, complete, on time—they will never let you go.

2. Norms to follow to successful sales call:

a. Dress code: Dress conservatively and professionally.

b. Be practical: Start initially with small business or stores, who might not have space for a bookkeeper and can't afford one on a permanent basis.

c. Plan your strategy: Avoid pushiness. Try to market your skills in an approachable way.

d. Marketing: Make sure you provide accurate information on the services you are willing to provide and what they cost. Print out a list of services on stationery with your letterhead. Provide a sample of your work, that the client is interested in like a budgeting tool, sample customer bill, etc.

3. Get CPA referrals: Get to know CPAs via letter or by personal appointments, so that they are likely to refer work to you. A word of caution here, the CPAs more often refer clients who are too small or are "problems."

4. Client referrals: Once you do a good job for a client, ask them to refer to their friends or other similar business prospects.

5. Billing strategy

a. Base fee: Calculate your fee based upon the local CPAs' lowest rates (for client write-up work).

b. Vary your rate according to the job: Analyze, how organized or disorganized your client is in the bookkeeping records and base your fee on your level of work accordingly.

c. Work help: Hire an assistant instead of hiring an employee. Get an accounting intern from a local college to do their internship with you. They get excellent training, and you get an eager assistant at minimum or no pay.

6. Check the quality of your work. Clients and CPAs respond to top quality. Triple checking to see that everything is in balance.

Do a mini-audit before your work goes to clients or their CPAs.

7. Bill by the job v. by the hour. Avoid charging a flat fee until you do a client's work for two or three months. Often you might end up work too many hours for too little money because of an open-ended commitment.

Possible disadvantages:

Main Disadvantage: Since you are working on a fixed salary, your earning per month solely depends on your client base and your skill to market and attract new clients.

Time management: It takes time to do the work and additional time is required to find new clients.

Negotiating your own hourly or fixed rates, may not be familiar at early stages of work.

There is always a level of uncertainty about finding the next project, even if there is a huge market for freelance bookkeeping.

Bottomline:

Like in all other cases it's up to the individual effort to rise and shine.

3. Cleaning services

What is it all about?

Where there are people, there will be a need to clean. If there is a necessity to clean, then there are people willing to pay you to clean. There are many directions you can take this business.

Three main types and most demanding cleaning business are

- Domestic cleaner
- Commercial cleaning company
- Specialized cleaning business.

Startup is easy and requires little initial investment on your behalf.

Residential Maid service or Domestic cleaner: Nowadays there is a huge market for this type of cleaning as many of the dual-income families use cleaning services. Here you will be involved in cleaning client homes, usually while they are at work, and leaving before they return.

In starting a Commercial cleaning business, you will be required to hire staff, who will be involved in cleaning. While your role will be mainly on managing the staff, promotion your business and finding new customers.

In the case of specialized cleaning business, it all depends on the work you have specialization in. For e.g. if you are a domestic window cleaner, then you will clean windows on clients house, or if you are specialized in removing graffiti, then you will be working with various councils.

Advantages:

- For most cleaning businesses, there's no need to rent/buy office space as most appointments are made over the phone or on clients office/home.

- Organize and arrange your schedule, and do any other paperwork from home.

- No special skill is required as it is a job that all types of people can do unless you are in specialized cleaning business.

- A domestic cleaning business with no staff can be started more or less for free, as you use clients' cleaning products. You may need a small amount to market your business, but you can create a free website and meet people in person to cut even those costs.

- With a specialist cleaning business, you'll have to pay out for the various materials needed for your particular area, but prices will differ hugely depending on what this is.

- Starting a commercial cleaning business will involve high start-up costs because you'll need professional equipment, several staff members, and a vehicle to get the team and/or equipment to the clients' location. You'll also require a larger marketing budget.

***Ideal for you* if:**

If you are a person, who enjoys cleaning especially other people's messy stuff and get a kick out of making things tidy.

If you are a person who is happy to do physical work all day long, to work alone and to take orders.

If you are trustworthy and likeable - clients have to hand their keys over to you and not easily bored since you will be doing repetitive, non-thinking chores day after day.

Advantages

For domestic cleaning businesses, you don't need any more training than you have from looking after your own home.

Not needing to invest in training programs means a quicker return on your investment, and is why domestic cleaning businesses are preferable for those with a lower budget.

You are your own boss. Therefore, you make decisions on when you work and when you don't. You would enjoy the freedom of working when you want and being able to take vacation when you want

Strategies to Success

The first thing to consider when starting a domestic cleaning company is whether residents in the area you're looking at can actually afford to pay someone else to do their cleaning.

Also, study the market and competition pricing in your area.

Decide upon your marketing technique and get started as soon as possible.: If you're starting an office cleaning company, call around to see if your services could be required or if you're looking for domestic cleaning, then it's time to start knocking on doors. Distribute flyers and generally try to get your name out there. Leafleting and advertising in newspapers and magazines might help you win clients, but simply knocking on doors with price lists can be more effective - and much cheaper. Potential customers sometimes react better to a friendly face than an ad in the paper, especially if they hadn't considered hiring a cleaner before.

Get criminal records check from the CRB to help reassure clients you're trustworthy.

Encourage word of mouth. You need to be trusted so recommendations from existing customers will be your best marketing. Consider some kind of reward scheme, to entice existing clients to refer friends.

Give clients a couple of weeks notice if cleaning products are running low, so you're never caught short. Ask clients exactly what they want done to make sure you meet their expectations. You could offer different levels of service (with different price points) - extra for doing ironing or window-cleaning, for example.

Possible disadvantages:

Cash flow can be a big problem for a cleaning business, as often cash is meant just to be left on a table for you - and is often forgotten. Will you ask customers to pay you weekly or month-by-month? In advance is the safest option cashflow-wise, but not be so agreeable to clients.

The work is purely based on physical aspect and from day in and day out you are required to do a monotonous job

4. <u>Personal Chef:</u>

What is it all about?

A personal chef is a professional service offered by a person, who prepares at-home meals for clients in private households for a fee. Aside from preparing professional-quality meals, personal chefs also save their clients the time and effort needed to cook their own food.

Personal chef work can be categorized into two different types:

      a. For individual people or families
      b. For a small catered event

Individual people or Families

People especially career-focused individuals, those with special dietary or health needs, seniors and those who enjoy fine dining, need someone to help with their meal preparation.

Personal chefs are becoming a popular alternative for people that don't have the budget for a full-scale catered event or for people that hosting small events that don't require complete catering services. As a personal chef, you usually serve the clients, with multiple meals that are custom designed as per the client's requirements and requests. The responsibilities include creating a customized meal plan, shopping for all groceries, preparing the meal, and cleaning up the kitchen. Usually, the prepared meals are packaged in containers for the client and stored in the refrigerator or freezer to enjoy later. Some personal chefs also involved in preparing dinner parties and other special events, which means they are responsible for shopping, preparing the meal, serving the guests and cleaning up afterward. Some personal chefs work on a self-employment basis, while others find jobs through a company that offers an in-home cooking service.

Advantages

Be your own boss. This provides the added advantage of creating your own hours as well as controlling your pay rate that is to protect against making the error of getting paid too little for too much work. Better to become you own boss so you can control all the negatives that come with being an employee.
1. No formal training is required to start your own personal chef business.

2. Gives you more autonomy and independence, as you will likely be working solo, determining your own approach and making your own decisions with regard to food preparation techniques

3. Low overhead with low start-up costs and part-time operating hours.

Ideal for you: If ?

It's ideal for anyone who loves to cook and serve others.

If you have skills to plan and create a menu from start to finish for a dinner party or for people with special dietary needs.

Basic knowledge on pairing different kinds of food and beverages is also required.

Strategies to Success:

Promotion: Join business networking clubs and social clubs to spread the news about your service. Word of mouth referrals is essential if you are starting as a freelance personal chef.

Clients: Depends on you and your skills, to choose the clients varying from individual, groups, businesses, corporations, association and colleges.

Be Creative: Be creative and pursue opportunities if you want to work from home full-time. The key is to do every job well so that your clients can do your marketing for you while sending you repeat business.

Drawbacks or points to watch out for when starting a business

1. Market Ignorance:

Study the target market, any ignorance on your part in identifying and understanding of eating habits of various groups of people across age, ethnicity, may lead to failure.

2. Pick the Right Tools

Since you are going into the business by yourself, pick the right tools to succeed in the field. A good set of knives, utensils and cookbooks are essential.

3. Customer Service

Since you cook in other people's home and handle their food, make sure you are clean and neat, yourself and also in your work.

Be responsible and make a good impression with each of your clients and be responsive to all inquiries. One negative experience or review can ruin your business.

4. Complicated Recipes

You are in the business to make money, so a good rule of thumb is to choose recipes that are easy to prepare in terms of following the recipe, acquiring the ingredients and preparation time. Complicated recipes may require expensive ingredients and also may take too much time to prepare and cook.

5. Ignoring Special Dietary Needs

Always be aware of other people dietary restrictions. Many people are now dairy-free, vegetarian, vegan or gluten-free, just to name a few special needs. Centering your personal chef business around one of these niche categories may open up business possibilities beyond your own mealtime preferences.

5. <u>**Personal Trainer**</u>

What is it all about?

A **personal trainer** is a fitness professional involved in exercise prescription and instruction. They motivate clients by setting goals and providing feedback and accountability to clients. Trainers also measure their client's strengths and weaknesses with fitness assessments. These fitness assessments may also be performed before and after an exercise program to measure their client's improvements in physical fitness. They may also educate their clients in many other aspects of wellness besides exercise, including general health and nutrition guidelines.

Personal trainers are not just for stars and athletes. Every single person can benefit from working with a trainer. Personal training is truly an investment in one's own health and well-being.

Personal trainers typically become personal trainers out of a passion for being healthy, fit and active. It's a job that starts out with heart, motivation and a love for all things fitness

Advantages

When working for yourself as a personal trainer, you are in control of your schedule.

You don't have anyone to answer to, and you make all the decisions.

Selling a service is easier than selling goods when you are self-employed. This is because you do not have to stock your product and, since a service is really all about selling time, you can be more flexible with promotions.

Most rewarding part of being a personal trainer is that you get a lot of the credit for changing the lives of your clients for the better.

Strategies to success

Understanding basic facts:

Understanding of the business of personal training, why clients train, what they are looking for, how they want to be looked after and what they are trying to achieve.

Target a market based on your skills

Target a market that relates to your natural personality and skills and make a detailed outlined plan to sell and professionally serve that target market.

Ability to deliver the deliverables

Able to flawlessly and confidently deliver exactly what those people will most want just the way they want it.

Disadvantages:

Some people think weight-loss is simply for sale instead of something that must be earned. As a personal trainer, it's common to encounter clients who believe that you are solely the one responsible for their weight loss simply because they are paying you. These clients may be late for workout sessions or cancel appointments. They give little effort and do not follow their diet. It is your job to motivate the clients, but the clients must be truly committed to their goals as well. It's important to establish this up front before signing a new client.

You have to be on top of advertising, finding and signing new clients, printing contracts, establishing policies, scheduling appointments, creating logos and branding, buying equipment and covering overhead costs.

6 <u>Concierge Service</u>

A personal concierge service runs on the most basic of premises. People want things done but don't have the time to do them. But they're happy to pay someone to take care of their business efficiently and with a touch of class. Why not let that someone be you?

Why the booming demand for concierges and organizers? A big reason is that most people have accumulated so much stuff--both in the workplace and in their homes. Just glance at your desk or kitchen counter, and you'll probably see stacks of papers, bills, correspondence, etc. Taking care of all that "stuff" requires time and organization. Some people need help just to get organized; others could manage the paperwork if they weren't saddled with so many other chores. That's when they turn to professionals to help keep them organized, run errands, and see to it that business and personal obligations are met.

Who uses personal concierges? Everyone from the millionaire corporate chairman to the single mom with two jobs and three children under age 10. Employers in certain fields, such as insurance, banking and manufacturing, have found that offering help to their time-stretched employees can boost productivity, making this a workplace perk that benefits the business as well as the workers. For this reason, more employers are offering personal concierge services to their employees.

list of some of the services personal concierges can offer might help you come up with a few ideas for services you can provide to your clients:

- Pet-sitting
- Light housekeeping
- Waiting in line at the DMV
- Car repairs, oil change, car wash
- Gift-buying
- Plant care
- Picking up dry cleaning
- Running miscellaneous errands
- Relocation services
- Making travel arrangements
- Mail pickup
- Meal pickup; some chef services
- Dinner reservations
- Interior decorating
- Concert/movie reservations, etc.
- Grocery shopping

- Locating hard-to-find items and collectibles

Ideal for you if?

If you have energy, strong organizational skills, and, most important, a talent for customer service,

Advantages

- You can provide any combination of services you want.
- You don't need any special training or experience.
- You have the ability to form long-term relationships with clients.
- You are your own boss
- You can grow your business from low-investment marketing activities, such as word-of-mouth referrals.
- You may be able to offer your services on a larger scale to local companies who want to provide concierge services as an employee benefit.

Strategies to success

Finding Your Niche

As an aspiring personal concierge, you need to decide what your niche will be. For instance, will you cater strictly to corporate clients? Will you specialize in particular areas for clients or offer more broad-based services? Some personal concierges specialize in one area, such as lining up tickets for concerts or special events; others pride themselves on running every errand imaginable. You need to spend some time thinking about what type of service you want to provide.

Start up material:

You need a computer and other office basics. Since it's a service-based business rather than a product-based one that calls for inventory, starting a personal concierge business doesn't require a large financial investment. In fact, much of what you'll need to be a good concierge can't be bought--for instance, the contacts that come from long-term business relationships with the right people. You can't put a price tag on those contacts, but having them puts you well on the way to success.

Pricing your services and Marketing

Once you've decided on your niche, focus on pricing, advertising, and how you'll run your service on a day-to-day basis. Consider joining a concierge association, such as the International Concierge and Lifestyle Management Association or National Concierge Association, or find a concierge network in your area.

Disadvantages:

You may have to deal with demanding clients and a demanding schedule.

If you are accessing your clients' homes, you should have insurance and/or become bonded to protect yourself from liability.

You may be busiest during your own busy season, such as holidays.

You may have to be "on-call" for clients who need last-minute assistance.

7. <u>Home Bakery</u>

Desserts make everyone happy, and you are happy by selling these desserts. It is a business that can be started from your own home kitchen. It translates from baking to family and friends to retail sales. If you've got a knack for making delectable desserts, consider starting a home-based bakery. You can offer your desserts for delivery or pickup, parties, and sell them from stores and online.

Ideal for you if?

You love to cook and spend every free hour in the kitchen, spatula in hand, flour covering your face. You have heard your friends or family tell you adamantly, "You should start your own bakery!"

Advantages:

You'll have a job you love, and you get to taste test... everything!

You'll work from the comfort of your own kitchen, thus the ability to work from home

Your own bakery business can be started with some business cards, flyers, and an armful of samples, thus low advertising costs

Starting your own bakery business doesn't have to entail all that preparation. You may already have everything you need at home, so low start up cost

Depending on your schedule, you can bake all day or bake at night, in turn providing flexibility of time

Work at your pace and accept the orders that you are comfortable to work with.

No employer or employee headaches. You'll be your own boss and the freedom that comes along with it.

Low-risk business, even if you fail it hurts your ego more than your financial situation

Creativity and a chance to show off your skills gives more than job satisfaction.

Strategies to Succeed:

Get information about the rules and regulations governing cottage food industry in your area? Also, study the cost analysis, market and marketing strategies.

- Legalities: make sure the Health department in your State allows you to operate a home bakeries
- Certifications, Licenses, and Health Requirements: Get all the required proper licenses and certification, based on your area and state policies. State regulations may also require owners of home bakeries to pass health inspections. Another certification you may be required to obtain is a food safety certificate
- Costs: Come up with a thorough business plan that includes your goals and costs. Costs include start-up costs and also ongoing costs like costs of basic ingredients etc.
- Target Markets: Choose your products based on the specific market you target. Your target market, the population you are catering to, is probably one of the most pertinent aspects of your business plan. For example instead of Danishes, go for cookies, cupcakes, muffins and bagels, which you are sure of selling to school students.

- Marketing: Do your research, get an idea of your surrounding target market such as schools, offices and even family run restaurants to sample your products and gain orders. Sell your products at local farmers market. Use of technology, create Facebook and Twitter accounts to market your products.

- Presentation and Packaging: Present your goodies in an eye –appealing way, to attract more customers. Always use proper packaging that will satisfy your customers

Common Problems faced:

1. **Getting good raw materials**
2. **Home baked products pricing**
3. **Hygiene and licensing problems**

Disadvantages:

1. Not only should you focus be on creating goodies but also on marketing strategies, as no existent market planning is a number cause for failure.

2. Baked goods are perishable items, so always have a backup plan for those items that are left over from sales.
3. Many large commercial stores may offer bakery items at a low cost, so it is important to price your home-baked product within a range that will attract customers.

8 Business Coaching:

What is it all about?

Is essentially helping or supporting entrepreneurs in start-up businesses or established business entrepreneurs to achieve success quickly and effectively, by helping them to improve their work performance through personal change. The most successful business coaches have plenty of experience in the business world, along with specialized expertise (e.g., marketing, finance, or sales). Whatever your niche, you need to have the ability to help your clients set and achieve their goals. Business coaching is also called executive coaching, corporate coaching or leadership coaching.

Business Coach plays many roles, but all is focused on creating a successful business. The role of a Business Coach is to coach business owners through guidance, support, accountability and encouragement. Business coaching helps owners of small and medium-sized businesses, to focus on the game by helping them in various fields such as their sales, marketing, management, team building etc.

Business coaching also teaches business on how to think through important problems that need to be solved in an enhanced manner, no more quick decisions and also on ways to work under pressure.

The major areas where a business coach improves performance in business are:

Productivity
Quality
Organizational strength
Customer service
Customer satisfaction
Keeping executives
Cost reductions
Profitability

Advantages of being a business coach:

1. Most of the coaching sessions take place via phone calls, so you can select clients regardless of their geographical locations.
2. You are again your own boss with that comes the freedom to work,

when you want and where you want to work and how to choose as your client.
3. There is no certification or licensing required being a business or executive coach, and membership of a coaching organization is optional.

Ideal for you if?

If you have the experience and knowledge to mentor a business

You enjoy teaching and love to help other people

If you are very patient, persistent and a determined individual as it takes a lot of time and energy to guide people.

And at last, if you are a person who truly cares about others and their business ventures, rather than just looking at your own bottom line.

Strategies to Succeed:

Experience and Expertise

The number-one thing that prospective clients look for is your experience. As a coach must have walked the walk. Clients look for people who have an experienced failure and made their way towards as their insight will help them avoid making costly mistakes and increase the chance of success immensely. Make sure to give testimonials and get references from your mentors and former clients.

Do not provide a long list of services rather be specific in the area of subject, in which you can provide your expertise based on your skills and knowledge.

Attitude and willing to share

Make sure you are willing to share both good and bad experiences with prospective clients. Be transparent and be persistent and determined in your attitude at the same also be patient.

Accessibility and Connections:

Be accessible and discuss the details about your time schedule and the commitments that you can provide and stick with it. Clients also look for the connections you have with other business ventures so that you will be willing to open the doors for them. So make sure you have adequate and appropriate business connections.

Expectations

Make sure to learn what a client expects time and action wise. Be accountable and make sure the deliverables are delivered on

Disadvantages:

Personality conflicts with a client about the differences in ideas than help to improve the business. Make sure your ideas are presented in a clear and understanding way so that there are no confusions in future.

Goal conflicts with clients on what or how on which target are achievable within a time span. Again emphasis on focus on deciding upfront what the goals are and the ways to achieve them

Scheduling conflicts, as a business coach, some clients may require being hands on all the time to discuss even about a minor detail of their business venture. Make sure to discuss the details of your time and schedule with your client and your availability in case of any emergencies.

9 Child Care Services:

What is it all about?

Child Care or Daycare is the caring and supervision of a <u>child</u> or children, anywhere from age six weeks to age thirteen. It is essentially an action of looking after someone else's child/children.

Since the number of working parents is climbing, it creates an ever growing need for quality child care. The Child care services can range from small home-based operations to large commercial centers. Here, we are discussing about a small scale investment in creating a job for oneself.

There are two major types of child care on a small scale investment basis

1. Licensed home day care or family child care: Here care is provided in the home of a caregiver who is licensed and regulated. They are small in size and provide families

with the same security as a day care center but also has the benefits of flexible hours, lower costs, accessibility, and cultural compatibility.
2. Home care or Babysitting: It is temporary caring of a child or children at their home. The type of work depends upon on the agreement between parents and babysitter. It can vary from watching a sleeping child, changing diapers, playing games, preparing meals, to teaching the child to read or even driving them to their classes.

Ideal for you: if

It's for people who love children and want to build a business caring for them. Also be a people person, have a high tolerance for stress, have good insurance, and have some management skills. Also be a very responsible person as the children are in your custody, you are responsible for their safety and well-being.

Advantages:

- You have a passion for helping young children and their parents.

- You enjoy the independence and responsibility of being your own boss.

- You have the time, knowledge, skills and motivation to make a small business succeed.

- You can save on your own child care costs.

- You can be home with and care for your own children.

- Tax Breaks: Home daycares probably have better tax breaks than any other at home business. Not only can you deduct the cost of the percentage of the household that's used for the daycare, but you can deduct food, gifts, toys, clothes, office supplies, transportation and schooling as it pertains to the daycare. That means if you use 100% of your house for the daycare, and it's open 24 hours, every home bill you have is tax deductible.

Strategies to Succeed:

1. **Type of service, you wish to offer:**
   Decide on the services you'll provide and the policies that will guide your operation.

   Different types of operations are:
   Family care -- A program designed to provide care for toddlers in the homes of other mothers.
   Home care -- A nanny or sitter cares for and supervises a child in the child's home.
   Day-care and child development centers -- Programs designed to respond to the stages of physical, emotional, social and intellectual growth and behavior of infants and children. Child care development home -- A private residence for up to five children, with no more than two infants in the group.
   Infant care center -- A child development center that cares for infants and toddlers (children two years old or younger).
   Before- and after-school care -- A program providing care for school-age children before and after the regular school day in a child development center or home. !

Satellite child development program -- A private residence linked with a child development center or an agency that receives technical assistance and support, training, recruiting and placement.

Nursery school -- Usually a part-time preschool child development center operating during the school year.

2. Identify the existing services in your community or area:

When assessing what child care services are already available in your community, ask the following questions like

What type of care exists in the community?

What age groups are being served -- infants, toddlers, preschool, school-age or combinations of the above?

Are there age groups that need more care than others?

What hours do the centers open and close?

What types of services do they offer? -- Daycare? – Night care? -- Evening care? -- After-school care?

How many centers are there?

Where are the centers located?

Is there a waiting list for child care services?
Are more centers needed in the same area?
What service can you provide that other centers aren't offering?

3. **Guidelines or license:** Check with the appropriate regulatory agencies to find out what's involved in providing that particular services, you have decided to go along.

4. **Marketing:** Be professional and when starting the business, get referrals from your family and friends to build your reputation as a child care specialist.

5. **Setting price and payments:** Consider a variety of issues, including the start-up costs, the profit you want to make, the going rates in your area and what the families you're targeting can afford. Setting your rates, explaining--and often justifying--them to parents and then collecting the money are all part of being in the child-care business. You may also want to consider, what

forms of payment, like cash or check, you are willing to accept.

Disadvantages:

- No Sick Days: Always have a backup plan to deal with the days when you are sick. You being sick don't mean the parents of children can take their day off from work.

- Communicable Disease and Illness: All types of potential issues may arise, as you are inviting your home to a multitude of children. The health issues may range from common cold, lice, flu, measles and chickenpox to name a few.

- Lack of Privacy: Your life will be an open book, as you are responsible for caring for other people children. Each and every part of your life can be scrutinized

- Constant Planning: You need to constantly plan, modify your schedule and program to be on top of the game.

- Collecting Payments: It is one of hardest thing part of running a daycare, as parents can be late in picking up the child from anywhere 5 minutes to an hour. So have a contract, which explains the terms and conditions to cover such lapses and not be taken advantage of your services.

10. Computer Service and Repair

What is it all about?

All modern-day companies require a wide range of IT services to maintain their smooth operation, and no IT service is more vital than computer service and maintenance. Without proper IT service management, computer systems break down or lose a significant part of their operational abilities, effectively limiting the effectiveness of a company. For that reason, frequent and dependable checks and repairs must be conducted, to ensure that all computers within a company are in optimal condition.

Computer services or repair is a fastest growing industry as almost all business and home offices nowadays use computers and depend on them to be working properly. People don't always have the skills, the time and desire to do their own computer service, repair or upgrades. Thus you can turn your PC prowess into a business.

Computer service and repairs also involves:

- installing new IT systems
- upgrading existing hardware and software
- visiting home users or offices to set up their PCs or fix faulty equipment
- testing systems to make sure that they are working properly
- preparing cost estimates for new installations

Advantages of home-based computer service and repair:

You do not need formal qualifications if you have a good enough working knowledge of computer systems and software.

You have a lot of flexibility in your choice of work that you want to provide.

The job opportunities in computer support are always on the rise, so you may never go out of work.

You can receive clients anytime of the day according to your schedule.

You also have the ability to choose what work or projects you want to tackle.

Save on overhead costs and space rental.

You are your own boss, and you have the freedom that comes along with it.

Ideal for you, if you have

- thorough knowledge of operating systems, hardware and commonly used software
- good communication and customer service skills
- excellent problem-solving skills
- a patient and organized approach

- the ability to meet deadlines
- a willingness to keep up to date with IT developments

Strategies to Succeed:

Street (and hourly) value knowledge:

Nowadays it's all about selling hours. Since you are making money by selling management services, get a clear idea about your billing rates on the hour basis. Investigate and get information on what the local competition is charging.

In cases of jobs, where you need to order new parts, make sure that the purchase worth yours and your client's time, especially if they have pre-paid you. Also remember to factor in shipping, handling and insurance costs, as well as an "opportunity" cost for ordering parts from lower-priced national vendors vs. a local supplier.

Customer base:

It all depends on what type of job you want to do. If you want to remain one on one operation, then ideally residential and small business clients may suit your needs. There is also an added advantage that residential work is less demanding, and the market for it is huge.

Managing time and knowing your strength and weakness:

Make sure to be available to take calls, as in this area, if you are not around to take the calls, the client just moves on to another guy from Yellow pages. Know your strength and weakness, for g. if you have a strong technical background but aren't very knowledgeable on the business side of bookkeeping or accounting, then either hire a part-time accountant to handle the business side of work and also invest in a good software product like, AutoTask, ConnectWise and Results which can help you manage people, projects and processes more efficiently.

Marketing

Make sure to market your service daily. You can choose your marketing ways from direct mail, pamphlet drops, telemarketing or web marketing

Update your skills

Update your technical skills and your knowledge of the latest and newest software that's available on the market.

Disadvantages:

Customize your workspace. You'll need a clean, dedicated workspace (not the desk that the family PC rests on) with room for a repair bench area for your tools and easily accessible storage shelves and bins.

License requirements: Getting a business license and obtaining general liability business insurance may be expensive depending upon your geographical location.

11. Debt Collection Agency

What is it all about?

Debt collection agencies are companies that are hired by people who want you to collect debts owed to them by business or consumer customers. With scores of people falling behind on debts, now's the perfect time to start a debt collection agency, which requires little more than a phone and a computer. You'll help retailers, hospitals, and credit card companies recover money they're owed, and in return, you'll get a percentage of the collected debt.

A debt collection business can be quite profitable and can operate from your home or a small business office. The most important imperatives for a debt-collection business owner is obtaining customers and then finding the debtors. As a debt collector you will be sorting out payment plans, recording payments that are made, organizing customer files (every job has paperwork and admin), chasing debtors and late payments and tracing debtors who move without telling the company (with the help of credit bureaus, telephone providers and even the post office). Also in some cases when creditors can't collect on unpaid accounts, they often sell them for pennies on the dollar to third-party debt collectors. The seller hands over spreadsheets containing bits of information on debtors. But frequently, those bits are outdated or inaccurate. So collectors have to play detective, searching databases, calling neighbors and contacting family members to get recent contact details so as to go and collect their money.

Advantages:

Low start-up investment: As a debt collector you can work from your own home with the basic requirement being a computer with internet connection and a telephone.

Be your own boss and work at your own pace and time.

Anyone can work as debt collector; the minimum qualification is a high school diploma.

Ideal for you, if

You are a good listener: When speaking to a debtor, it is important to listen to why they are in debt. This will help the debt collector determine a solution.

You are a skillful negotiator: Working with debtors to start some sort of payment plan or outright repayment of debt requires good negotiation skills.

You are good speaker: Debt collectors spend most of their time on the phone talking with debtors.

You are a very persistence person: Some debtors do not want to be found, or may not be responsive when called by a debt collector. Successful debt collectors do not take no for an answer.

Strategies for success:

1. Need to fully study and understand the Fair Debt Collection Practices Act.
2. Also know about local regulations, such as licensing according to the state you want to work as a debt collector.
3. Additional training or a degree in business or finance may add credibility
4. Before starting your company, it is vital that you work with a debt collection agency first. Here you can see how the entire process works and get some hands-on experience on working as a debt collector. Aside from on-

the-job training, becoming a member of two professional organizations are great sources of support and information.

5. The International Association of Professional Debt Arbitrators (IAPDA) offers online training courses with the purpose of obtaining a certified debt specialist certification. The IAPDA also offers online support and the newest available online education tools. The Association of Settlement Companies (TASC) lobbies on behalf of debt collection companies and ensures that its members are practicing fair and ethical debt collection.

6. Design, or hire someone to design, brochures, signs, business cards and letterhead for your debt collection business. Write a letter to local businesses that may need your services and introduce yourself. Use company letterhead to print the letter and make sure the letter is clear, concise and

grammatically correct. Call local businesses to make appointments with owners and offer your services.

7. Obtain a collection attorney to support your agency in its endeavors. A collection attorney assists you in limiting your liability and increases your success in debt collection. If legal steps need to be taken, your lawyer helps you secure a judgment against the debtor and protects and enforces the rights of your creditors.

Disadvantage, if any?

May need to make around 150-200 calls per day, as most of your main work is done via phone calls, it can be monotonous and cumbersome.

It's a high-stress job, and the hardest part will be if people can't pay their debts at all, because when this happens, it's your job to follow the law (and court procedures) to get the money. This can involve working with solicitors and even bailiffs, so expect tears, tantrums and a lot of swear words.

12. Dog Walking

What is it all about?

Another in-demand service in the pet industry is dog walking. Dogs need daily exercise, and many pet owners hire dog walkers to ensure their pooch gets enough. Dog walkers take pooches out for their daily constitutional one or more times a day, either individually or in small groups. In some cities across the United States, like New York, dog walking alone can be a booming business. But it's actually more common for dog walkers to offer additional services, including playing with and feeding pets.

Advantages:

- Though dog walkers, of course, have their appointments they must meet but it certainly is nowhere near like a stuck up 9-5 schedule, and it also is often much more pleasant to speak to the four-legged doggy clients.
- Exercise in fresh air, dog walkers have their exercise built-in their job~ killing two flies with one swat!
- You can be your own boss and have your clientele based on your time schedule.
- The startup cost is very low.
- You can walk more than 1 dog at a time, often in groups, generating more income.

Ideal for you, if

Of course, it's a known fact that you should be a dog lover.

You are also nature lover

You love to walk and take care of animals

Strategies for success:

To manage groups of dogs that belong to clients in busy parks and trails might need specialized knowledge, so sign up for a course and learn about dog behavior, managing a pack, fight prevention and basic first aid for dogs.

Most dog walkers offer various services, including full one-hour walks, shorter walks, individual and group walks and short 15-minute breaks, all at different prices. Set the prices for the services offered and this will help to project and plan your daily routine and income.

Insurance is needed as it will also cover a dog walker if the grip of the dog's leash is lost and it attacks another dog or person. Most clients will expect dog walkers to have insurance to protect themselves and their pet.

Register the business and get a tax identification number.

Take out liability insurance coverage especially if a client's dog bites someone or sustains an injury while in the dog walker's care. Several insurance companies offer membership along with property damage insurance for pet-related businesses, some for as little as $100.

Join local dog walking associations. Organizations such as the San Francisco Dog Walker's Association, for example, have ethics and recommendations for their members to follow, and membership will help build the credibility with clients.

Market the dog walking business. Have fliers printed advertising with credentials and the services offered, and ask the local pet stores and other businesses to display them on their counters. Let the local and personal veterinarian know that he can refer clients to your business.

Build a webpage with services offered and send the link to family and friends, asking them to pass it on. List the business with the national directories such as Dog Walker and Pet Sitters International.

One can also join companies like 'Zingy' which have apps for pet owners to directly hire the services offered.

Disadvantages if any?

- The sun isn't always shining when going on the job or it is shining a tad bit too much. Dog walkers are out there in almost every kind of weather, no matter if rain, sunshine, icy cold or hot as long as it is in the goods of the dogs.
- Dog walkers cannot call in sick as easy as it might be working an office job. They are caring for living beings, fur kids who look forward to their walk and need to go outside for potty.
- Clients moving away. Each dog takes a piece of a dog walker's heart with him!

- Definitely not the nicest part of a dog walker's job is to pick up poop along the way!

13. Home sewing business:

What is it all about?

Sewing is a great skill, and there are ways with which one can make money with it. If you already have knowledge about sewing, then it will be a very low start up job. The most important step is to start right, and one way of doing that is looking at a person's talent and hobby and looking into how to use it to make money.

Everyone loves a personal touch and identity that handmade things have. Since the whole world loves personalized gifts especially handmade ones, the handmade crafts industry is in a boom. Handmade items never become old. If they last, they become vintage pieces and even heirloom pieces. This makes them even more precious.

Advantages:

There is always a market for handmade items.

You are your own boss, and you can work at any time and place of your own choice.

You can be creative and innovative in your designs and make money out of your talent and skill by working from home.

There is a range of sewing specialties to choose from according to your talent and market needs.

A very low start-up job, especially if one knows how to sew. Basic requirements include a sturdy sewing machine (not an expensive one!) and threads and needles.

Entails little or no overhead, and propagates itself entirely by word of mouth.

Ideal for you? if

You are someone who has flair with using the needle.

You love to create new designs and play with fabrics.

You love to stitch, darn and mend clothes.

Strategies for success:

First part is to choose one of the sewing specialties that one is capable of doing. A few examples are

Alteration and Repairing: The most basic of sewing businesses and also very high in demand. Almost everyone has something that gets in the need of alteration or repairing over time. A great percentage of garments require alterations even when bought brand new. Retail garments are sold in fixed sizes. Many people would love to have a good tailor who can fix the clothes to their requirements. It is a kind of a sewing business in which you can charge a high per hour dollar rate, which means more money for less work. This type of work will require knowledge from darning to re-fitting, working with different fabrics and stitches etc.

Custom Sewing: Becoming a dressmaker and make dresses and clothes according to the client's specifications. They can range from dresses, casual wear, or formal wear. This type of work requires knowledge on latest in fashion, trends, styles and create garments with good finishing.

Bridal Sewing: Custom bridal dress sewing is not only a great business idea, and they also generate a lot of amount of cash. Every bride likes individual attention and customization so that the bridal dress is unique and special.

Sewing home and craft Items: One can sew a lot of things in and around the home like bags, table mats, kettle covers and stuffed toys.

Once it is decided what type of sewing specialization one is capable of doing, then choose the machine and set up business according to the choice

The trick is not to stop learning new things and improving constantly.

Research the basic groundwork. Known what is in demand at around the area you live and your competitors and their rates? Also might need information about business permits, traffic considerations, sign regulations. Check if there are any zoning restrictions in your area that prohibits hanging a sign on one's own property.

Given that this is a people business where one really need to see his/her customers (e.g. fittings, consultations, etc), determine the rules in terms of traffic. The neighborhood zoning rules may prohibit constant comings and goings of people into the home based business.

Keep track of customers, and the time taken for completion of a project and also the time taken for acquiring patterns, fabrics and other accessories. All the details and the market analysis of your area will help in deciding the pricing your sewing services. Try and establish a decent hourly wage and also calculate a fixed benchmark for certain common and similar jobs.

Possible Disadvantages:
Sometimes clients might now understand the intricate job and the time it takes to complete the work so, they might not be willing to pay for additional hours you had worked on their project.

Custom designing especially bridal dress may be time consuming and might require last minute alterations, messing up your work- time schedule.

There will always be dissatisfied clients, who might not be willing to pay for the job already completed.

14. Lawn Mowing

What is it all about?

It's the art of cutting grass in a lawn by making the lawns look attractive and healthy. Many a starry-eyed entrepreneur have thought that they could start a mowing service because "how hard could it be? I know how to cut my own grass." But without proper planning and research, one is likely to face failure. So make a plan of action before venturing into a business.

As lawn maintenance is a seasonal business, with downtime during the winter in about two-thirds of the country. In fall, one can offer services for winterizing lawns and raking leaves and during the winter, offer services like snow plowing, to maintain cash flow through the year.

Lawn maintenance services are required by:

- Homeowners who are frequently out of town on business
- Affluent homeowners, who don't have time for proper lawn care.
- Retirees who don't care to do their own maintenance any longer
- "Snowbirds" with winter homes in warmer climates
- Golf course managers who may need help with maintenance
- Rental property or condominium association managers who are personnel-impaired

- Facilities managers for botanical gardens, historic buildings, municipalities and other government entities, universities, cemeteries and other public places with green spaces

Basic facts about lawn mowing:

Basic lawn maintenance consists of mowing, edging and trimming. Often, bush and hedge trimming is offered as an extra service, but it's more time-consuming and requires more manual dexterity than mowing.

Mowing height and mowing frequency determine how healthy and attractive the lawn looks.

Most grasses have a range of recommended mowing heights. Stay at the upper end of that range when the lawn is under stressful conditions, such as hot weather or drought, or if you have a shady lawn. In cooler weather, you can cut the grass a little lower.

Follow the one-third rule. For a thriving lawn, never cut away more than one-third of the grass blade in any one mowing.

Edging and trimming are pretty close to being the same thing. Some tools are called edgers because they're designed to trim the lawn along a hard surface like a driveway or sidewalk. Edgers cut a nice clean edge but leave some dirt and grass debris that you need to clean up. On the other hand, you can use trimmers anywhere — along a hard surface, in tight spaces, next to planting beds, and so on.

Grass clippings are valuable organic matter, chock-full of nitrogen and other nutrients. As long as you often mow enough to remove no more than one-third of the grass blade, the easiest thing to do is just to leave clippings on the lawn. The pieces break down quickly and reduce the amount of fertilizer you have to use by as much as 25 percent.

Advantages:

There are many advantages to running a home based lawn care or landscaping service. You're master of your own destiny, and you can devote as much or as little time to the business as you want. You have a short commute to work if you're based in your own community. You can work at your own pace and at virtually any time during regular daylight hours. You also can enjoy the fresh air, get a good cardiovascular workout, and bulk up your muscles.

The price of all this freedom and body contouring is relatively low. Once you invest in the tools and toys you need to manicure lawns or install landscaping professionally, you're generally set for years. You don't need much in the way of office equipment, either, and you can set your office up in the corner of the den or a spare bedroom rather than laying out extra cash for a commercial space.

Ideal for you, if?

You love the smell of cut grass and a genuine love of the outdoors and growing things. It's what drives them to spend most of every day on the job covered in dirt.

If you like working outdoors and are capable of doing heavy lifting and handling machinery and hazardous chemicals such as weedicides and pesticides

Strategies to success:

Need to have more adept at mowing, trimming and pruning than the average person which means learning gardening basics and techniques.

You have to be physically fit and able to handle the rigors of the job, which can include lifting heavy equipment off and onto trailers, and wielding bulky handheld implements for hours at a time.

It's crucial to the survival of a business to keep all the equipment in peak working condition. That means cleaning the mower blades at the end of each day and using a grinding wheel regularly to keep them sharp. Safety while working and make sure to take every precaution possible to protect oneself while working. Always wear safety goggles and ear protection, and always remember to let your mower cool down completely before you gas it up.

Another important part of the job is providing estimates to prospective clients and establishing prices before making an estimate. Knowledge on how much to charge per square foot and knowing competitors rate helps you make your business a success.

Disadvantages, if any:

- **Seasonal:** Many weather factors also affect the work such as storms and tornados other than lawn mowing being a seasonal job.

- **Competitive:** If the market is too oversaturated, then there will be a need to compete off price, and this will cut into gross margins.

- **Some Economic Risk:** When economic times get tough, existing residential customers may find the need to cut non-essential expenses, and for many, outsourced lawn care is one of those.

15. **Wedding Planner**

What is it all about:

A wedding planner is a person who helps in designing, planning and management of other people weddings. A wedding planner organizes things for the bride and groom so that they have their special day without much stress. Couples who work long hours and have little spare time available for organizing their wedding typically use wedding planners.

The typical services of the wedding planner includes:

1. An interview with the couple to find out about their needs
2. Preparation of budget that fit into clients needs
3. Designing the event
4. Scouting for venues

5. Preparation and planning a detailed checklist which includes, attendee lists, venue map etc.
6. Helping the couples select and hiring wedding professionals and service providers such as photographers, caterers, videographer, beautician, baker, florists etc.
7. Help the couple to in preparation and execution of the contracts and coordinate the delivery/services during the big day
8. Preparing a backup plan in order to run the event in a smooth way and also to be a successful one.

Ideal for you, if

Your organizational skills are top notch, you thrive under pressure, and you have a flair for putting together beautiful events, think about becoming a wedding planner.

You have an eye for detail and love parties, weddings and other events, consider becoming a wedding planner.

You're people person and have patience and skill to deal with frazzled brides.

You have knowledge about how to manage finances and budgets.

Advantages:

It takes very little to start up.

It's creative and challenging, with a lot of split-second decision-making.

It can be done on an hourly basis according to your time schedule, and one can pick and choose the clients you want to work with.

It's a job where you are your own boss, and you get to work at your own time and place of your choice.

It's a business that will exist as long as mankind exists.

Disadvantages/Challenges

Must be very organized to ensure that they will not be any disasters on the big day.

Need to be creative to attract prospective clients as the wedding planning business is a very competitive market.

Should be able to advise the bride and groom on what they can get for their budget and provide them with resources and price ranges for everything from invitations and photographers to orchestras.

Lastly, since weddings are emotional for everyone involved, it's vital to stay cool, help soothe ruffled feathers and suggest compromises.

Strategies to success:

Should be able first to prepare a budget and also be able to manage a budget.

Establish a relationship with local wedding-oriented vendors--florists, photographers, bridal shops, videographers, caterers, hotels and country clubs, bakeries and cake decorators, jewelers and musicians.

Take a certification course, example like the one offered by [Association of Certified Professional Wedding Consultants](#). A degree in hospitality can be helpful for event planners, but short-term certifications from organizations like the International Special Events Society can also be useful.

You can also gain experience by planning weddings and parties for friends and family. Market your business through ads in the local Yellow Pages, in the society or wedding section of your local paper and in special bridal supplements.

Leave your brochures with all contacts and ask for referrals

Also consider hiring an attorney for basic legal work, such as protecting your personal assets from liability and drawing up basic contracts you can use with your clients before you take on their wedding.

Create an online portfolio which includes:

- A photo shoot of a mock wedding, including the reception table, decorations, and the cake. This is a chance to show off your familiarity with the hottest wedding trends and your attention to detail. Use this as an opportunity to work with local vendors. Offer to give them referrals in exchange for contributing to your mock wedding.
- Written testimonials and pictures from your friends and relatives' weddings to which you have contributed.
- A list of your certifications or professional memberships.
- Samples of wedding timelines you have created.

As a small business owner, you'll need to wear many hats. You'll be not only a wedding planner but also an accountant, a marketing director, and a customer service specialist. When you pull off a successful event, you'll see the hard work will be worth the challenge.

16. Yoga Instructor

What is it all about:

It's undeniable — yoga is a trend not only with the younger generation but also with the aging population, as seniors benefit from low-impact workouts. According to Yoga Journal analysis in 2008, more than 14 million Americans have been recommended to practice yoga by their doctors. Yoga is attractive to today's price-conscious consumers who don't want to spend a lot of money for exercise equipment.

Yoga instructors guide students in yoga practice. They help students learn poses and use the correct forms. Yoga instructors may also provide guidance in yogic philosophy as well as areas complementary to yoga, such as nutrition and meditation. Yoga instructors may work full- or part-time, and some are self-employed. Depending on their employer and yoga class schedule, instructors may work daytime, evening, night, weekend or holiday shifts. Travel isn't uncommon, whether it's among several locations of a gym or to clients' homes.

Advantages

With the growing popularity of the practice of yoga, there is always a job in the market. Flexibility in working time schedules and be own your boss

Also, your own health is taken care of, when helping to take care of other people's health and wellness

Also get to inspire people to live in a more holistic and harmonious manner. The best yoga teachers are those who are charismatic and able to influence others to make profound changes in their overall lifestyles.

Ideal for you, if

You are interested in careers involving fitness,

You are concerned about wellness of fellow humans

You are into healing and spirituality

Strategies for success:

One important thing to take into consideration is the fact that transitioning from a yoga student to a teacher is not an overnight change and may take between six months to a year to create a strong base as a teacher.

Sense of openness and a commitment to deepening one's yoga practice is the best way to prepare to serve future students. It is essential for those interested in teaching yoga to understand that doing so is a life-long journey that involves continually evolving and learning new aspects of the practice to share with others. Even after years of experience and advanced certification, many yoga instructors report how they are still always learning new things about the practice.

In addition to being a constantly deepening experience, teaching yoga is much more than simply demonstrating yoga postures. Teaching yoga is a new art in itself that requires one to speak flowingly through the class, not sound boring, deliver the right cues, provide the best adjustments and give the best verbal instructions to help students learn the poses with ease.

Think carefully also about what style of teaching will feel most authentic for you personally, as well as the amount of money you can realistically spend on a teacher training.

One more important consideration for prospective yoga teachers is that simply completing a teacher training program is not always adequate to prepare you to teach. You will often need to practice teaching with an experienced yoga instructor who can give you feedback on your performance. Time spent with this teacher can help you refine what you learned in your training and make it your own, as well as help familiarize you with the demands of teaching yoga. Consider purchasing insurance as a next step in getting started as a yoga teacher. Low-cost insurance for yoga teachers is available through Solana Beach, California's Fitness and Wellness Insurance Program. Members of the Yoga Alliance, Kundalini Yoga Teachers Association and the California Yoga Teachers Association can get special insurance rates.

It is also a good idea to prepare a student information form if you plan to teach independently of a yoga studio. This form should include information about whether a student has practiced yoga before, what other physical activities he or she does and about any medical or chronic conditions or injuries.

A waiver would ideally accompany the student information form and include an agreement from the student to take responsibility for not exceeding his or personal limits in yoga practice and for any discomfort or injury he or she may experience.

The most common way to market your classes is to create a flier or business card. You can post your flier or card on car windshields, in mailboxes and on community bulletin boards in local restaurants, cafes and grocery stores. You can drop your fliers off at local hotel concierges and include handouts with your drop-in class schedule. Other good places to leave fliers and/or cards are the waiting rooms of chiropractors, body workers and other complementary medicine practitioners. The Internet is another great marketing tool. Consider creating a website for yourself as a yoga teacher. WordPress, Blogger and Yahoo are just a few sites that provide web hosting at relatively inexpensive rates of $20 or less each month. If you prefer having your own domain name, you can visit GoDaddy.com to find out what is available. Social networking sites like Facebook, Twitter and Linked In are other great virtual places to advertise your class offerings quickly. These sites give others the opportunity to ask you questions regarding your classes and share the information with their friends and family members.

Another idea for attracting potential yoga students is to offer to provide a free workshop to organizations like nurses' or teachers' groups or parent teacher associations. You can volunteer to teach for free at your local library or hospital as a way to introduce new people to yoga and possibly build a following.

Word of mouth is a great way to advertise, so referral incentives and free classes for first-time students are another great way to attract new students. New yoga teachers can offer discounted or free classes to new students and those who refer others to them if they teach independently of a yoga studio.

Disadvantages, if any:

Driving all over town to teach a class: When considering any job, don't forget to add into the cost to you, which are reflected in the time to drive back and forth.

This can increase your overall expense and time. If you have a schedule that requires you drive all over, it can lead to increased cost and frustration.

Knowing how to market your classes and workshops: Knowing how to be an effective marketer of programs is essential in order to grow the business.

Finding you don't have enough time in the day to also practice yoga for yourself: Most teachers don't do the entire sequence with their class, if at all, and even if you did some yoga with class, it's never the same as practicing on your own or taking a class. As a teacher, you'll need to practice what you preach and make your own practice a priority, being creative around how and when you'll do your own yoga.

Managing illness, injury and scheduled days off: Need to be cautious about anything that might cause injury and be organized and also taking care of one's own health.

Having jobs end or losing jobs-sometimes unexpectedly: Sometimes, despite the best efforts, jobs end or sometimes classes in studios are discontinued due to low attendance.

Managing your time between teaching and administrative time: All yoga teachers have to divide their time between teaching and deskwork. One also needs time to managing finances, marketing, business development, public relations and developing program content, all while one is also teaching yoga.

17. Online-Tutoring

What is it all about?

It is the process of tutoring via online. Teaching in a virtual environment or networked environment, where the teachers and students or learners are separated by time and space. A lot of college and schools offer online courses nowadays as a secondary educational tool, due to the immense popularity of the Internet within schools and businesses.

Online tutoring is one facet of teaching that is becoming more and more popular. Utilizing employees who work from home is becoming more commonplace among mainstream companies. Online tutors are now a very popular way for parents to find qualified teachers to help their children in specific educational areas. The advantages of on-line tutoring for students are one on one attention, individually tailored lessons and focused learning are just to name a few.

Advantages:

- **Flexibility.** To a significant degree, online teaching jobs allow you to set your own schedule. You can complete most of your work whenever and wherever is most convenient for you – as long as it gets done within a reasonable time frame. Details vary depending on the type of class and your employer's expectations, but most online teachers enjoy the freedom to decide when they read and grade assignments, how they pace their lesson plans, when they respond to students, and how they monitor online discussions.
- **Transcending barriers.** Ideally, online education creates rich learning interactions that defy boundaries of race, class, geography, physical challenges or other differences. With some online teaching jobs,

you have the opportunity to connect with students from all over the country – or even the world. Many online teachers thrive by facilitating lively discussions and debates that might not have been possible without technology.

- **Helping students who need it most.** Online teaching is a great alternative for students who don't thrive in a traditional education atmosphere, who want to accelerate their learning, or who need to take classes that are not offered locally. Many online teaching jobs serve students who can't access traditional education; they may be geographically isolated or unable to attend school due to illness, pregnancy or other challenges. There are even online teaching programs, such as Westwood Cyber High in Detroit, that focus on re-engaging dropouts and at-risk students.

- **Growing web-based teacher network.** Some teachers fear being isolated by online teaching. But there's no need to worry: there are many growing communities of teachers supporting one another online. Popular websites like TeachAde facilitate social networking and resource sharing between teachers all over the country and worldwide.

Ideal for you if:

Love teaching, (goes without saying), For teachers and work professionals, who want to make a difference and want to work in the ever-rewarding field of education while earning supplementary income from home and enjoy the flexibility of the home work environment.

Strategies to success:

More than one way to become an online tutor:

1. Online tutoring companies because they companies provide Software, tools and lesson plan materials to tutors in addition to helping tutors find students. Researching online tutoring companies is essential. Many of the tutoring companies have different requirements (teaching certificates, experience requirements, specific references or background checks), so finding a company where you are most likely to be hired is a good place to begin. Also, research carefully to be sure the online tutoring company you are interested in joining is well established. Most companies charge a fee for connecting with their pool of students and for gaining access to online teaching materials. Be sure that any money you put towards an online tutoring company is legitimate and that the company will provide you with fair pay, access to

students, good materials and also hires only qualified individuals.

While each company's qualifications will be different, experience is almost always a must. Additionally, qualifications change based on the subject tutors are teaching as well as the grade level they wish to tutor. It is best to look up each individual company's qualifications to see if your tutoring skills are sufficient. Most companies require any of the following:

– Knowledge of the subject

– Teaching or tutoring experience

– IT and Internet skills

– A relevant degree in the subject you will be tutoring

– Relevant qualifications above the level you wish to tutor

– A diploma in Teaching

– Certificate or Postgraduate Certificate in Education

– NVQ levels 3 or higher in Learning and Development

– Other special certificates for non-teachers who are qualified to tutor

2. Freelance, are a well-established teachers or tutors, but it will still require software and forums that online tutoring companies provide free of charge to member-tutors.

Challenges of Online Teaching

Online teaching does require some special effort and preparation. Here are two key areas in which you may need to improve your skills if you choose this career path:

- **Planning and preparation.** To overcome the challenge of connecting to your students without looking them in the eye, many experts agree that online teaching jobs require at least ten hours of preparation for every hour of online instruction. Online teachers must be prepared to teach effectively to a wide range of student needs.

Careful forethought also helps set the right tone for interactions between students.

- **Teaching students to learn differently.** In addition to teaching course subject matter, online teachers have to teach their students how to learn online. Most students aren't experienced in the online teaching environment. Frustration and poor outcomes may result if online teachers don't set clear expectations and provide the guidance students need to succeed.

18. Senior Care Services

What is it?

A growing population of senior citizens means big opportunity for non-medical home care providers, who help seniors with tasks of daily living. The services you offer might include transportation, house cleaning, dietary assistance, bathing, administering medicines, and, perhaps most important, companionship.

The different types of senior care services can be:

Relocation service Many people in the rapidly growing 70-and-over population segment are selling their homes in favor of smaller houses or condos either in traditional neighborhoods or retirement communities. This is a perfect time to cater to the relocation needs market.

Moving is always stressful, and it can be especially traumatic for someone who is leaving a home they've been in for decades that is full of precious memories. Adding to the challenge is the fact that families are more spread out geographically and not always available to help with the moving process. Not only is the packing and cleaning process physically demanding, it also takes an emotional toll. A senior relocation consultant can provide an element of compassionate objectivity as decisions are made about what to keep, give away, sell or toss.

As a senior relocation specialist, you can offer a wide range of services. It's typical to provide a total turnkey package, which means you'll orchestrate every aspect of the move, including:

- Assistance with selling the current home
- Assistance with finding a new residence
- Assistance with selecting a moving company
- Sorting and downsizing
- Estate sales
- Coordinating movers, utilities, cleaning and other tasks
- Packing and unpacking

Home care and home healthcare services. Seniors and family members of older relatives are looking at alternatives to assisted living and nursing homes. The best option for most is home care or home health care, where a professional caregiver goes to the home to personally look after a loved one. This may include doing laundry, picking up around the house, reading the newspaper out loud and preparing meals. Most important, this service includes companionship--someone who adds conversation and friendship to the life of an elderly person who is homebound, physically impaired, has difficulty getting around or just may be lonely.

Concierge service. In the corporate world, concierges are often referred to as personal assistance. They perform a wide range of services for clients. A concierge who targets seniors performs many similar functions with a twist: Their mission is to enrich the lives of their elderly clients by delivering services that allow those clients to maintain an independent, dignified lifestyle as long as possible.

Seniors turn to concierges for things they can't or don't want to do for themselves. Some of the concierge services you may provide include:

- Companion/support
- Administrative assistance
- Organization of closets, cabinets, basement, attic, garage or filing system
- Errand and courier service
- Mail delivery and pickup (if mailbox isn't at residence)
- Grocery shopping
- Personal shopping
- Fitness training
- Computer training and support
- Daily checkups
- Reminder services
- Cleaning services

- Pet care services
- Meal preparation

    Transportation service. Nondriving seniors often rely on family members or neighbors for transportation, but these resources aren't always available. Many community transportation systems, such as public and paratransit (specialized transportation service for persons who are unable to use regular public transportation due to a disability or health-related condition), are not considered senior friendly because many seniors can't walk to a bus stop, can't easily get into or out of a van, or can't afford a taxi. Seniors need reliable, comfortable transportation with sensitive, responsible drivers who will wait for them at the doctor's office, escort them when shopping and running errands, and most important, be where they're supposed to be on time so the client is not left waiting.

Advantages:

You are your own boss, and you get to pick and choose your clients according to your schedule and family situations.

You get the satisfaction of helping people in need. It's a great feeling to take care of other people especially elderly people. Knowing that you provide a much-needed service for those who are in poor health or in their declining years can be an extremely gratifying way to make a living.

The startup and overhead costs of starting a senior care business are very low.

It's a growing industry as many elderly folks now want to live out of their own home instead of moving to a facility.

Ideal for you, if

You love and desire to help people especially elderly people

You have to be a people person and have very good judgment dealing with people and the issues surrounding them.

You need strong management and entrepreneurial skills, if you plan to work directly with seniors, you also need:

- *Honesty and integrity.* You may be trusted with access to your clients' homes and sometimes even to their bank accounts.
- *Patience.* Even the sweetest, best-natured client will have a bad day, and you need sufficient patience to work through it.
- *Versatility.* Often, providing services for seniors necessitates wearing more than one hat at a time. Be flexible and willing to shift gears at a moment's notice.
- *Interpersonal skills.* You need to enjoy being around seniors and not be bashful about making conversation. At the same time, you need to be a good listener. Many seniors like to reminisce about earlier times

in their lives, and they have some truly interesting stories to tell.
- *Reliability and punctuality.* Your clients will appreciate being able to depend on you to pick them up on time or keep appointments as promised.
- *Compassion.* You need to be able to demonstrate understanding and encouragement with seniors whose capacities are failing.
- *Knowledge.* You can be a tremendous asset to your elderly clients by having information about various services available to senior citizens, both locally and nationwide.

Strategies for Success:

Determine what type of services you can provide. The first step is to decide what you, or those you hire, are physically capable of providing. Will you offer only a visit and meal preparation? Other services to consider include light cleaning, reminders to take medication, feeding pets, accompanying the client to social functions, companionship and transfer assistance.

Obtain the necessary permits and licensing and that will depend on the state you are living in and where you want to work.

Obtain training in CPR. Family members tend to feel more comfortable leaving their loved one with someone who has emergency training and knows how to respond in a tense situation. Also, basic knowledge about medications is added benefit.

Obtain insurance. Although most of the homes where you will work most likely have homeowner's insurance, it is a good idea to obtain an umbrella insurance policy that will cover you personally in case of a lawsuit or injury.

Set your prices. Since senior care is a service business, you won't have a lot of overhead. Driving to locations and advertising are the two big costs. Decide if you will offer a discount for regular bookings, multiple days in the same week and the maximum distance you are willing to travel.

Market your business via fliers, local advertising and also by social media and by word of mouth by friends and family.

Disadvantages, if any?

Need to make sure that one is health so that they are not susceptible to any sickness when caring for elderly people.

Sometimes the work schedule like doctor visits can be time consuming, so plan your work day schedule accordingly.

19. Translation Service

What is it?

Language translators are in big demand these days. International commerce is growing as fast as the internet, and while we may believe that English is the world's linguistic choice, it's not. So people who can translate documents from one language to another are in high demand.

If you are fluent in a foreign language, you can earn a living as a translator. Although some translation services are now handled by technology, human translators are still needed for good quality, accurate translation.

As a language translator, you'll interpret all sorts of documents, from books to private letters to product labels, but your greatest source of revenue will be legal and medical companies.

Advantages

There will always be a need for human translator despite the technology advancements in language translation software field.

The advantages to this business are that you can work at home as part time, and you'll deal with all sorts of interesting people and materials.

It's a great home-based business, especially because you can work via the Internet. Overhead costs are very low, and you have the potential to make significant profits.

You have a very broad target market, including legal, commercial, medical, technical editing, interpretation and more. The cost of startup of a language translation service is relatively very low.

Ideal for you, if

You are fluent in more than one language and can efficiently translate from one language to another.

You like the nuances of languages; it's always fascinating for you.

Strategies to success

Write a list of the services you want to offer depending on your knowledge and also on the market situation in your location. Write down all services you are confident you can provide to customers at a professional level. As a freelancer expect, many of your customers to be from the legal and medical fields. An understanding of medical or legal lingo is also a plus so that your translated materials come out sounding like the real thing.

Certification as a translator is a plus but not a necessity

The quality of the translated material is key. No business wants the embarrassment of translated materials that have errors or even worse, contain mistakes that could be culturally offensive. Businesses know that communications with their customers have to be right. They're not willing to take the chance on a bad product and they're willing to pay more for that assurance.

You will need a definite fluency in your specialty languages.

You'll also need good administrative and organizational skills.

You should get a good picture of the market situation you are about to start working in and especially with respect to the place you are working at. You can also target book publishers, government institutions like welfare agencies and immigration services, insurance companies, and import/export firms. Send direct-mail brochures to targeted businesses. Place ads in trade publications and introduce yourself to supervisors and administrators at local hospitals and institutions. Adjust the prices according to your expectations, location and market situation.

Possible disadvantages:

Some of the potential challenges of starting a translation business include:

- You must have complete and thorough command of whatever languages you plan to offer translation services for.
- Among your competition may be computerized translation programs and voice recognition technology.
- It can take some time to establish the business, depending on your location.

- You may want to become certified before offering your services.
- You may possibly need transcription equipment if you will be doing audio translation from tapes.

20. Photography

What is it all about?

Photography is a vast world. There are many different types of photography and many different kinds of people that enjoy it. Photos are so special because they give people memories of times and places and events in their lives. People always hold onto these memories forever with a photograph.

By capturing the special moments in other people's life, one can make a living out of it.

One can make money as a portrait, event, or wedding photographer.

Advantages:

You actually get paid for your photographs! And you can pick and choose the assignments you want.

You work solely for yourself, selling each photo or series of photos individually. You are your own boss.

It's a very exciting profession

Ideal for you, if

You love photography

You're skilled with a camera and have a mind for business,

Strategies for Success

Build a Portfolio: Build a portfolio with samples of work.

Create a good website with a daily blog: The website is going to be a most important ally. It is what most people will look at when considering a person for a job

Tricks for great photography: It's the quality of the photo that will determine the job and payment. It takes more than just point and shoot to get a great photo. Learn about focus, lighting, colors and backgrounds and much more.

Keep learning: The investment of getting a Lynda and/or Kelby training account and these educational, video-based resources taught by highly qualified and amazing teachers, will add value and keep you updated.

Quick repose to job offers: Get the dialogue going quickly or else the person starts to look elsewhere.

Job searching and Marketing: Some cities have photography groups that meet to share photos and tips. There are also many groups online dedicated to photography and freelance photography. Also start submitting the photos for contests and magazines. Get a list of photography markets and start submitting photos.

Disadvantages, if any:

Keep in mind that starting a photography business requires substantial capital for lighting, cameras, lenses, and photo-editing software, in addition to normal business expenses.

Aside from skills and equipment, there will also be marketing costs like developing a cutting-edge website, social networking, and mailers.

The freelance photography life can be hard. Long hours for little pay, alone with no co-workers to speak to or have lunch with, the lack of stability of a weekly check.

21. Arts and Craft instructor

What is it?

People enjoy learning arts and crafts. When you think of craft instructors, usually the images that come to our mind are painted pinecones, woven bracelets, and a finger painting or clay pinch pot. Well, crafts go far beyond those simple stereotypes. Craft instructors teach people things like candle making, soap making, weaving, pottery, carving, silk-screening, photography, woodworking, sewing, and glass blowing, among others. Arts instructors teach knitting, painting, print-making, sculpture, stained glass, pottery, glass-blowing and woodworking. Arts and crafts are one field that people are willing to shell out their hard-earned money to learn.

Advantages:

Arts and crafts can be taught from anywhere, from home based studio.

Can teach all over the world via internet based video sessions.Creative entrepreneurs may even choose to film and broadcast their training classes via the internet to a worldwide student base, without any travel.

You are your own boss.

The start-up cost of being an art or craft instructor is less, as an established or expert arts or craft person, you may already have all the material in your hand.

Can make money by teaching and training persons a profession which you have mastered. The options are nearly limitless when you have a skill that other people are willing to pay to learn.

Arts and craft which never goes out of market, therefore you have a steady market for business.

Might have a wide range of students from kids to adults, so get you to meet people from all walks of life.

Ideal for you? If,

You have mastered and have vast experience with various handicraft projects utilizing an assortment of materials.

You like imparting knowledge to other people and like teaching.

Have Exceptional knowledge of art concepts and theories

Have Strong familiarity with various artists and artistic methods

An In-depth knowledge of art history especially the 18th through 20th centuries

Should have excellent ability to perform multiple tasks efficiently

Should possess very good written and oral communications abilities and astute observational skills

Strategies for success

Promote your classes through arts and crafts retailers, by running advertisements in the newspaper, networking at business and social functions, posting notices on community bulletin boards, and by exhibiting at arts and crafts shows.

Also using social networking websites to promote your classes.

Choosing the rates will depending on how many people are in each class, material and equipment requirements, and the art or craft being taught.

Make a plan of lessons according to the strength and capacity of the students.

While the important points to note while teaching are

- Course methods and routines that are clear to the teacher and student
- Varied and appropriate teaching method and materials
- A supportive, cooperative atmosphere
- Enthusiasm, energy, caring, and maintenance of a non-threatening atmosphere
- A manifest belief that their subject is important
- Relates instruction to student interests
- Content expertise
- Assess the student achievement

Disadvantages, if any?

Sometimes students may quit classes in the middle of a session for varied reasons.

Make sure you also charge for the materials that you for teaching sessions.

22. Information consultant

What is it about?

The amount of information available today is staggering. For companies planning new products and patents or scoping out the competition, and for many other types of businesses, the trick is in figuring out how to access the information they need. In the past, information consultants were generally ex-librarians or full-time librarians who moonlighted by doing extra research for clients. Things have changed a lot in the past 10 years. Now, primarily due to easier access to information online, information consultants can come from virtually any profession. Medical receptionists can become medical researchers. Magazine editors can become expert researchers in topics they used to cover in their magazines.

Paralegals or legal secretaries can take their knowledge of legal matters into business doing research for lawyers. It's even possible for you to become an information consultant without any experience in the field by subcontracting work from established consultants. The possibilities are endless. Why, then, isn't everyone with any sense doing this type of work? The answer is simple: Many people are just not cut out for it.

Advantages:

In this technology age, you can work from home and be your boss

Most of the businesses nowadays require some kind of information and ready to pay to get this information, to succeed in their field. Therefore the area to gather information are endless and according to a person's subject expertise and experience, one can choose which field to start working as an information consultant.

Collecting information has become such a big business that in some areas--especially the fast-moving high-tech world--there is a large enough market for specialized information that some consultants make their living by researching specific topics and offering their findings for sale on the Web. They use the information itself to attract customers. Some even collect data on specific industries and charge customers a subscription price to receive weekly bulletins via e-mail.

Many companies don't have the resources to do their own research. They may also not need research done regularly enough to justify taking on an employee to perform it. It's generally far more expensive to hire an employee and provide the needed equipment and benefits than it is to hire outside help.

Ideal for you, if?

Some questions that help one person to realize if they are cut out for information consulting:

- Do you like to read?
- Do you like research?
- Are you a "people person"?
- Are you a logical thinker?
- Are you organized?
- Are you disciplined?
- Are you self-confident?
- Are you computer-literate?
- Can you handle the financial demands of starting a new business?

Strategies to success:

A few types of clients that always look for information consultant are:

- **Lawyers looking for the historical background of a particular type of case.** Lawyers constantly need to sort through old lawsuits to find precedent-setting decisions. Smaller firms are more likely to need outside help with this task. This type of information consulting is particularly fitting if you have a background in law--if you've been a paralegal or worked in the research department of a large legal firm, for example.

- **Corporations looking for information on competitors and potential suppliers.** Believe it or not, many large companies really aren't all that knowledgeable about their competitors. Some will hire you to find out everything from the specifics of another company's product line to figures that show how profitable a company has been over the course of the past few years. Some use this information to make sure they remain competitive, and others use it to scope out potential strategic partners, suppliers and even companies to buy.

- **Companies or individuals looking for patent information.** There's no reason to reinvent the wheel, right? That's why many companies hire information consultants to find out about potential patent and ownership conflicts. This is an especially important subject for high-tech developers, whose ideas may be considered intellectual property even if they're not patented.

- **Magazines compiling buyer's guides.** If you've ever seen a 50-page buyer's guide in a magazine, chances are it was put together by an information consultant. Most publications don't have the time or the resources to put together a complete listing of products and services for their readers. This can be a good place to start for information consultants with knowledge of a particular industry.

- **Publishing companies looking for untapped markets in hopes of**

starting new magazines or newsletters. Publishing companies, especially ones that publish several magazines that each serve niche markets with small numbers of subscribers, are constantly trying to identify new markets. Once a new market is found, the search for competitors begins (to be sure there's a need for a new publication), and research is conducted to find out whether the market is valuable enough to warrant launching a new publication.

- **Investors seeking company background information.** Sometimes the stock market numbers don't give the entire story, and providing financial and historical data on companies can help investors decide where to spend their money.

- **Individuals looking for personal information.** For reasons that range from checking the truth of someone's resume to locating a long-lost relative, people often want to find personal information about other people. This type of research is performed for clients that include lawyers, private investigators, employers and even people digging into the pasts of potential spouses. Researching personal backgrounds is not for the faint of heart. While the information you're providing to the client is generally available in public records, there's no guarantee that the client's intentions are honorable. Before you start conducting personal research for clients, be sure to talk to a lawyer about potential liabilities.

Again marketing and promoting your job is very important aspect

Established information consultants rarely turn down a job--even if it isn't in their particular knowledge niche. It's entirely possible that another consultant may hire you as a subcontractor based on your background or skill set. While the client may not know who you are, it's a foot in the door and a great way to get experience.

Once you've picked an area of expertise, test your research skills by finding contacts at companies you can provide services for. Call them up and introduce yourself. If they've never hired an information consultant, just knowing that someone is available may entice them to use your services. As you engage in this little exercise, you may be surprised by the number of companies that enlist the aid of information consultants.

Another way to find out more about the market for information in your area of expertise is to join an organization such as the AIIP. This kind of organization gives you access to people who have years of experience as information consultants. The AIIP also provides a listing on the internet where you can display your area of expertise and find others who do similar types of research.

Disadvantages, if any?

The important disadvantage is that sometimes, you'll be pulling your hair out trying to find information that doesn't seem to exist.

Client might not like the information you provided and might refuse to pay for your services. Make sure you have a contract and also make sure you know the exact information what the client wants, make them spell it out.

23. Medical Transcription

What is it?

Medical transcriptionists listen to audio recordings of medical records, such as doctors' notes, X-ray reports, and discharge summaries, and transcribe them into a word processing program. Medical transcriptionists take dictation and transcribe, listening to recordings made by physicians and writing the information given into medical reports, records, general correspondence, or other administrative material. Depending on the medical transcriptionist's place of work, the documents he or she transcribes may include anything from patient medical histories to autopsy reports, patient exam notes, hospital discharge summaries, and more.

Advantages:

Because they perform a necessary function, medical transcriptionists are always in demand. Skills are high in demand. Demand for skilled and qualified medical transcriptionists continues to increase as the healthcare field grows rapidly. There will always be jobs available for medical transcriptionists.

Startup is with a low overhead — you'll need a computer, Internet access, a printer, headphones, medical dictionaries, and a foot

pedal and software for audio playback —
this business is easy to start.

One of the biggest advantages of being a medical transcriptionist is that you can work from home. Many stay-at-home parents and those who work at a part-time job outside of the home find that this type of job offers more flexibility than in-office positions and is also very rewarding. **Those transcriptionists working from home may have more flexible hours, working full or part-time, and may also work more irregular hours, including evenings and weekends.**

You are your own boss, and that's definitely a plus point

Working independently. Most medical transcriptionists to work from home or in an office and are independent contractors. This means they can set their own pay rates and work schedule, and may be able to work with several different clients. Many get to be their own boss, and can enjoy an unlimited income potential throughout their career.

Easy certification and degree completion process. Medical transcriptionists can complete training that lasts between six months to five or more years, depending on the level of education they want to complete.

Ideal for you, if

You are knowledgeable on a variety of topics: medical terminology, legal issues, anatomy, and more.

You possess excellent vocabulary and grammar skills, as well as computer knowledge,

You have a strong attention to detail, fast typing skills and are willing to learn some medical terminology

Strategies for Success

A medical spellchecker helps, and you can get a system for rapid text entry, such as Instant Text. Find out about training and connect with others in the field through the Association for Healthcare Documentation Integrity.

Medical transcriptionists are not required to become certified, but many choose to do so. The Association for Healthcare Documentation Integrity (AHDI) offers a number certification options for medical transcriptionists. Many vocational schools, community colleges, and [distance-learning programs](#) offer medical transcription programs, usually, a one-year certificate program or two-year associates degree, often with on-the-job experience included.

Option to specialize in a field. If you want to work exclusively for a specific type of doctor or healthcare practice, you can specialize in a certain field and earn a higher than average income.

Disadvantages

You must be able to listen and type at the same time, and quickly.

Missing Out on Workplace Relationships and Social Relationships:

> Since you are your own boss with full freedom, which ought to be your greatest enemy unless you are strictly self-disciplined, you will find it difficult tackling lethargy.

Missing the General Trend in the Industry: Due to lack of oral communication at job between colleagues, you are bound to miss the current general trend in the industry. Maybe attending some trade shows or conferences could get you some rough ideas on what is going on in the industry, but overall you will be void of the latest news pertaining to the industry.

You are at Risk of Becoming a Workaholic: On your chase for money, you end up becoming workaholic. The mind equates each and every minute wasted to money lost leading to working up to 16 hours a day and would further end up working even on weekends.

Missing Employee Benefits: As an employee, you enjoy all those statutory employee benefits like minimum wages, stipulated working hours, paid holidays, health insurance, health checkups, etc. However, you could only dream of a paid holiday if you are an independent contractor!

24. Tour Operator

What is it?

Tour operators devise, arrange, and promote holidays and travel options, working with hotels, airlines and other transport companies for ground travel, in order to execute the arrangements. This promotion is either done through travel agencies or direct to the customer by means of brochures or websites. They provide customers with advice on where to travel as well as the best means of reaching such destinations.

Typical tasks carried out on a daily basis by a tour operator include:

- Providing general and specific advice about different travel destinations
- Drawing up complicated travel itineraries and ensuring that all the needs of the customers are met
- Making arrangements for transport, accommodation, tours, and activities
- Contacting airlines, hotels, and ground transport companies such as coach operators to make suitable arrangements
- Advising the customer about travel issues including required documentation and financial matters, such as appropriate exchange rates
- Using the computer database to research information about hotel accommodation fares and hotel ratings
- Dealing with payments
- Performing general administration tasks
- Dealing with and documenting complaints in an efficient and diplomatic manner
- Planning and advertising different promotions

- Making alternative arrangements for customers who have had their trips interrupted by unforeseen issues
- Evaluating customers' holidays and issuing appropriate feedback forms
- Making presentations to travel groups

Advantages:

You are your own boss and choose what type of work or specialty you want to focus on.

Tourism is an ever-growing industry, so you are never out of a job.

You have access to a variety of discounts, special rates, insider information and travel offers that help them provide the highest levels of expert advice for their customers but also for your own vacation. Some establishments provide heavily discounted or even complimentary stays at hotels around the world. Hotels and hospitality chains are happy to extend discounts with the hopes that they will enjoy their stay and recommend it to their customers.

Low start up as you might need only a computer and web connection to get all the information required.

Ideal for you, if you have

- Love for travel and gathering information
- Knowledge of key holiday destinations
- Foreign language skills
- Excellent interpersonal skills
- Communication skills
- Customer service skills
- Organisational skills
- IT skills
- Commercial awareness

- Good time management skills

Strategies to success:

The Product. No amount of marketing will help sell a bad product. Even if the product is great, it is not going to compensate for poor pictures and descriptions. The most important thing here is great photos and videos that inspire and catch attention

Pricing. Make sure to check out the competitors pricing and in case if quoting a higher price make sure the customer knows why.

Selecting platform for selling your product: In the case of selling day tours you can get a Tripadvisor page and for selling multi-day tours you can try Trustpilot, Facebook or Google+.

Social Media Marketing. Start with Facebook, G+, Pinterest, Youtube, Linkedin and Twitter after you have a product with reviews. Rule number one is to be interesting and stop thinking only about promoting yourself. Post great pictures, answer questions, create conversations and have fun.

Tour and Activity Distribution Sites. Check out and get connected to local and national tour websites.

Responding to Customers. The average tour operator takes more than 24 hours to respond to the initial email from a potential customer. This is way too long. Respond within an hour if possible and make sure to address specifically whatever issues the customer has posed.

Disadvantages

One of the major disadvantages is that it depends on the economy and in the case of low economy, there might be lack of clients.

25. Legal Transcription

What is it?

A legal transcriptionist transcribes speech or audio files of legal proceedings into written reports. Legal transcriptionists, often known as court reporters, record in writing the exact speech of legal proceedings, business meetings, and public events to accurately capture what is said by attendees and create permanent files. You will be transcribing client interviews, court hearings, depositions, interrogations, and more. Working for law firms or legal service agencies, legal transcriptionists may also store audio files and be responsible for the distribution of reports to clients, the media, and other sources.

Legal transcription has come into the public view recently being recognized for its efficient and professional influence on legal records and is steadily becoming a popular trend in the legal field. Legal transcriptionists, much like their counterparts in the medical field, listen to dictations from legal professionals and type them into documents that are edited and grammatically correct. These transcriptionists generally listen to testimonies, interrogations, court hearings, and pleadings, after which they compose what they heard into an easily understood document that will turn into a record.

Legal transcriptionists generally work for larger firms or private practice attorneys who have a large number of cases. They are also widely used by large corporations, governmental departments, insurance companies, and banks that all have a need for more accurate legal records. A large number of transcriptionists work for the U.S. government attempting to establish a more organized and complete record system.

After transcriptions are complete, they become legal records that are extremely useful to lawyers when they are researching to win a case. Thanks to these transcriptionists, legal records are now more clearly written and thorough. The lawyers and paralegals who wrote the records before were often too busy to make sure the records were exact.

The legal transcription field has not yet gained support from governmental organizations as medical transcriptionists have, but their role as newcomers to the business is likely to blame. Despite that, legal transcriptionists are steadily becoming permanent fixtures on law firm and government department payrolls and the need for their services will likely continue to grow even more.

Advantages:

The job market is unique in that there are little competition and plenty of jobs. Legal transcriptionists are hired by companies that choose to outsource the work for lower costs and increased quality. By outsourcing, companies will generally have a quicker turnaround rate as well because they are dividing jobs across the board rather than giving them all to one particular person.

Again you are your own boss

Work-at-home transcription jobs can offer a number of benefits. You don't have to worry about dress codes or rising early to battle rush hour traffic. Work-at-home transcription is also ideal for anyone who needs maximum scheduling flexibility.

No formal training is required to become a legal transcriptionist, and the start-up cost for setting up as a legal transcriptionist is very low.

A high school diploma and on-the-job training can be enough to become a legal transcriptionist.Programs are available in specific legal transcription technology methods, like stenography. Aspiring legal transcriptionists should consider taking classes in court reporting, legal terminology, dictation, composition, and grammar.

Ideal for you, if

You should have good hearing and listening skills

You have a solid understanding of legal terminology,

Possess excellent spelling and accurate typing skills

Should also have impeccable grammar and a good command of the English language.

You like typing work

Strategies for success

Although no formal training is required to become a legal transcriptionist, many companies require a basic knowledge of legal terminology and excellent grammatical skills. They also tend to gravitate toward individuals who have prior experience in writing, or an extensive knowledge of English.

Court reporters may need to pass a state licensing exam to be able to work in a courtroom. The Registered Professional Reporter credential, a commonly earned certification, is available through the National Court Reporters Association.

Top-notch typing skills are a must.

While legal transcription training isn't required, it will be an advantage as it provides knowledge of the legal terminology and legal formatting knowledge you need to succeed. Check local community colleges or search online for transcription training courses.

Promoting and marketing your services as legal transcriptionist is a must to attract clients.

Disadvantages

Sound quality, multiple speakers, accents, people talking over each other, and audience interaction can significantly slow down the transcription process causing frustration and reducing productivity

Templates provided by client may be difficult to work with

Transcription is not multi-tasking friendly; you will need to concentrate so no telephone calls or tweets

Real-time transcription requires that you and the client are available at the same time. This does not allow time for editing, or breaks

As with any task you perform for your client, you will need to ask some important questions before you get started. Need to make a checklist of some kind, because finding out certain information ahead of time will save you time and aggravation

<u>26. Social Media Consultant</u>

What is it?

Businesses need help managing their social media presence. In particular, they need to tweet on Twitter and post on Facebook in order to raise awareness of their companies and promote their products.

A social media consultant is essentially the eyes, ears and voice of a company online. That means you need someone who can raise the brand awareness, deliver traffic to a website, and boost the bottom line -- all while keeping the company's reputation top-of-mind.

Have you learned how to use Twitter and Facebook? If so, you've qualified to call yourself a consultant.
Now that you know how to use Twitter and Facebook, you can use it to build your social media business. But first, you need proof that you rock. You need to show your

potential clients you know what you're doing.

- You need 10,000 followers on Twitter
- You need at least 500 friends on Facebook
- You need 100+ Connections on LinkedIn
- You should start a blog and write at least once a week. (Only write about the success of your business)

How do you do all that? Just go out there and start following and friending as many people as you can. Tell them all you're a consultant.

Advantages

With more companies and organizations looking to hire social media help, and more social-media-savvy, there are more opportunities to work as social media consultant.

Startup cost? Zero.

Ideal for you, if?

You have social media knowledge

You like marketing

Having an avid interest in digital is a must, as the technology that drives social media is constantly evolving

Strategies for success

Learn a little more with online tutorials on how to become a social media consultant. Then contact everyone you know to see if they need this valuable service.

Social media consultants run the gamut from those who define strategy to those who implement it or build systems to maintain it. There are coaches, community managers, researchers, and technologists. The trick is finding what YOU have to offer and putting it out there. Is there a need your skill is set and if so, where? What services would you like to provide? What sets you apart?

Begin with one area that interests you, whether it's fashion, travel, technology, green living, or your local market. Learn everything you can about that niche and target those types of businesses. Over time, you can branch out and leap into other areas of interest, but it's wise to keep you focus small while you are and grow as the opportunities arise.

Another way to find clients is to offer webinars or classes. Develop content and materials on social media and put them in front of people who most need your help. Seek out and offer to speak at conferences or industry events within that niche.

Pricing is tricky since it depends on many factors— type of client, scope of work, duration of project, etc.

Building your brand goes hand in hand with building your business.

Disadvantages

Social media marketing is very hard work as it is about marketing and not social media

It takes an enormous amount of work to become "known" and attract customers. Be prepared to put in long hours every day.

Business especially small business expect immediate results from their marketing dollars

27. Online Retailer/E-Retailer

What is it?

It is a form of electronic commerce which allows consumers to directly
buy goods or services from a seller over the Internet using a web browser. Alternative names are e-web-store, e-shop, e-store, Internet shop, webshop, web store, online store, online storefront and virtual store.

Due to lack of time, nowadays, most people shop online for various things, without leaving their desk or home.

Advantages

Easy access to market - in many ways the access to the market for entrepreneurs has never been easier. Online marketplaces such as eBay and Amazon allow anyone to set up a simple online shop and sell products within minutes.

Reduced overheads - selling online can remove the need for expensive retail premises and customer-facing staff, allowing you to invest in better marketing and customer experience on your e-commerce site.

Potential for rapid growth - selling on the internet means traditional constraints to retail growth - eg finding and paying for larger or better premises - are not major factors. With a good e-marketing strategy and a plan a scale up order fulfillment systems, you can respond and boost growing sales.

Widen your market/export - one major advantage over premises-based retailers is the ability expand your market beyond local customers very quickly. You may discover a strong demand for your products in other countries which you can respond to by targeted marketing, offering your website in a different language, or perhaps partnering with an overseas company

Customer intelligence - ability to use online marketing tools to target new customers and website analysis tools to gain insight into your customers' needs.

Ideal for you, if

You have patience, diligence

You have knowledge on the right online business tools.

Strategies for Success

In fact, you can launch an e-commerce business with as little as a few hundred bucks. For instance, eBay lets you put up a store and find customers for your products for only around $20 a month with one of its online storefronts. If you want to strike out on your own, there are companies that sell professional website templates for about $100. For around $10 a month, a company like Yahoo! will host your business and provide email accounts and technical assistance.

But before you begin, decide what you want to sell. If you love tennis, consider selling tennis shirts or balls. If you're a car mechanic, maybe auto supplies are your thing. As for inventory, begin with a few basic products and add more selection as you scale up.

Whatever type of retail store you're starting, a good business plan is essential. Get ideas from this assortment of sample business plans for clothing stores, online stores, e-businesses, gift shops, eBay, art galleries, and other retail businesses.

The e-commerce landscape delivers a wide range of business benefits, including operating a store 24 hours each day. Delivering a simple shopping experience will keep customers coming back to complete purchases. For someone just starting, online retail business can provide a strong environment for building a business. Shopify offers a range of tools to help business owners start and sustain a successful business.

Writing an online retail store business plan requires several components that address the marketing, financial and advertising activities business owners will pursue.

Once the business plan is in place, business owners can identify the appropriate business structure. The Internal Revenue Service offers a range of helpful information that can assist people with selecting the appropriate structure. Once the business owner chooses a business structure, they must then file the incorporating documents with their state or county. This establishes the business as a legal entity.

Filing the documentation that legally establishes the business takes care of the offline process. Business owners can then choose an appropriate domain name and set up their website. Following the launch of the website, marketing and advertising efforts should begin, although many people build up a "buzz" about their products using social media tools prior to launching the website. The online retail store business plan should provide the foundation for developing the marketing strategy. Starting an online retail business also requires that business owners select the appropriate business model.

The online retail business model provides a foundation for delivering products to consumers and generating revenue. Online retail business opportunities are numerous and choosing the appropriate business model for selling products can make or break a business opportunity. For example, the e-commerce model delivers a catalog through a website that provides a shopping cart. The website serves as a catalog that customers can review and select items to purchase. The e-commerce online retail business model requires an online shopping cart solution. Shopify offers an e-commerce hosting package that delivers important tools, including email, a domain name and unlimited bandwidth.

Multiple online retail business opportunities exist and selecting the appropriate model depends significantly on what a business owner wants to accomplish and how involved they are willing to be. If a business owner is just starting, online retail business prospects deliver a range of moneymaking opportunities, from selling handcrafted products to sourcing products from distributors. For example, some business opportunities allow business owners to sell products and have them drop shipped if the business owner does not have a warehouse to store goods. Other opportunities require the business owner to house products, arrange for their purchase and manage the distribution process.

Disadvantages

- **Website costs** - planning, designing, creating, hosting, securing and maintaining a professional e-commerce website isn't cheap, especially if you expect large and growing sales volumes

- **Infrastructure costs** - even if you aren't paying the cost of customer-facing premises, you'll need to think about the costs of physical space for order fulfillment, warehousing goods, dealing with returns and staffing for these tasks

- **Security and fraud** - the growth of online retail market have attracted the attention of sophisticated criminal elements. The reputation of your business could be fatally damaged if you don't invest in the latest security systems to protect your website and transaction processes.

- **Legal issues** - getting to grips with e-commerce and the law can be a challenge, and you'll need to be aware of, and plan to cope with, the additional customer rights which are attached to online sales

- **Advertising costs** - while online marketing can be a very efficient way of getting the right customers to your products, it demands a generous budget - especially if you are competing in a crowded sector or for popular keywords

- **Customer trust** - it can be difficult to establish a trusted brand name, especially without a physical business with a track record and face-to-face interaction between customers and sales staff. You need to consider the costs of setting up a good customer service system as part of your online offering.

28. Mobile Pet Grooming

What is it?

People love their pets, but neither pets nor their owner loves the bathing and grooming process. In this busy world, they don't have time to take them to pet shops for their grooming, so with a well-equipped van, one can make a business out of it by visiting pets at their homes to bathe and groom them. It saves time and money going back and forth to the groomer.

It can take place in a van, motor home, trailer, etc. Service takes place in the customer's driveway or curb. It is outfitted in such a way so as to completely groom almost any dog or cat.

Advantages

Earning potential is excellent. The American Pet Products Association estimates that U.S. pet owners will spend nearly $51 billion on their pets in 2011.

Going mobile offers more freedom. Have the ability to set your own schedule

You get to work with animals every day you choose

You can charge more because this is a premium service.

No commercial real estate, minimal capital investment, no inventory, high client retention, low advertising costs, and the vehicle is a tangible asset to the business.

There is currently not any state requirement for being a Pet Groomer, so no rule or regulation to adhere to.

Ideal for you, if?

You are an animal lover

Have a great deal of patience and the willingness to master the craft.

You'll need plenty of experience in pet grooming, including the proper ways to clip and brush various breeds

You have knowledge of animal behavior.

You should also know something about human behavior.

Strategies for Success

It's absolutely necessary that you know how to handle frightened pets, who may bite or show other aggressive behaviors when it's time for their cleaning. Consider getting hands-on training at a grooming school. You can get answers to many questions by joining an online pet grooming community.

Since your clients will be dog and cat owners, you'll want to make the rounds of pet shops and veterinary offices with your brochures and business cards. Introduce yourself, leave your materials and ask for referrals. Place an ad under 'pets' in the classified section of your local paper and in the pet-grooming section of your local Yellow Pages.

You'll need a van (or an old but serviceable motor home if you already have one) set up for pet grooming with a tub, grooming table, generator or outdoor cords long enough to give you access to an outside power supply and, of course, all grooming tools and supplies.

Shelters have grooming departments, so this is a perfect place to begin! Offer neighbors, friends, family, etc. a free groom for the family pet to get hands on experience.

When going mobile, you will need to schedule a route. You do not want to be at one end of town one minute and then have to be on the other side the next. Schedule yourself so your appointments are close together. In the beginning, you will want to take everything that comes your way. Just schedule yourself so clients are somewhat close together.

You could also go by a flat rate, rate by size of the dog or by the number of dogs. Some mobile groomers charge an extra service fee after the third dog in a multiple pet household. You can have add-on services such as teeth brushing, facials, nails polished, etc. Learn canine massage and add this on. You can retail products as well out of your vehicle.

Disadvantages

Pet owners might watch your work and may be critical of your work

Some pets can show aggressive

29. Virtual Assistant

Businesses are looking to outsource key services, and instead of hiring full-time assistants, many are looking for virtual ones. As a virtual assistant, you'll perform office support duties, such as word processing, data entry, bookkeeping, and research, from your home.

Virtual assistants are independent entrepreneurs who work remotely and use technology to deliver services to clients globally. Most work from their home offices and receive their project instructions by phone, fax, e-mail or even instant message. Although many virtual assistants offer secretarial services, as more people with diverse backgrounds and skills enter the ranks, virtual assistants who specialize in such areas as marketing, graphic and Web design, IT support or even translations are becoming more common.

Clients are most likely to hire virtual assistants to save money-virtual assistants pay for their own equipment, taxes, training, healthcare and insurance or because they need help with a temporary project. Industries most often hiring virtual assistants include the real estate, coaching, financial services, accounting and legal.

The work can be very different with each client, but basic work areas include preparing reports, researching, editing, appointment-setting and many other services.

Advantages

Business trends forecast an increase in service demands,

Startup costs are minimal. You need a phone, a computer, and Internet access; you can be a virtual assistant (VA).

No more lengthy commute or the long office hours, to do the same work as a virtual assistant, or VA,

Self-employed and you can work from the comfort of your home.

Could have more than one client at a time depending on your own skills and efficiency.

Ideal for you, if?

You have a good marketing strategy

You are bright, efficient and organized,

You like doing the job of being a PA

You have good communication skills

You have basic knowledge on IT skills like MS word and excel and internet skill to do research.

Strategies for success

It is important early on to have a clear idea of the specialized services you want to provide and the target client audience you want to work for. If you start as a general VA with no real focus, then it will be hard to effectively distinguish yourself from other virtual assistants. Having specialized skills will make you stand out from the competition.

Depending on your experience level, you may consider taking a virtual assistant training course,

Connect with the virtual assistant community through the International Virtual Assistants Association and update yourself on what's out there.

The key to building a profitable and rewarding Virtual Assistant business is to align yourself with the right support network and mentors who will show you the ropes on how to grow your business.

You might want to consider joining a professional organization or networking group. This will give you the opportunity to network, build camaraderie and have access to a knowledge bank for solving technical problems.

Disadvantages

Many virtual assistants work between 14 and 18 hours a day during the startup phase. Even after establishing solid practices, one-third of these business owners admit working nontraditional hours, including weekends and holidays.

One of the downsides is there might not be constant workflow, and therefore pay does fluctuate.

30. Web Design

What is it all about?

Nowadays, just about every business needs an online presence. Everyone and anyone has a website, so the focus now is on the most innovative and exciting. Brands have to continuously refresh their websites. Whether it's through new design or the latest in interactive content, the current trend for innovation means that web developers and designers really need to keep up-to-date with the latest technologies and to keep the creative juices flowing in order to beat the competition.

Web design is as much a science as it is an art form. While half of the job is based on sound coding and design know-how, the other half is based on just having an intuitive sense of what looks good and what doesn't. Any web designer worth his salt will develop a strong core of fundamentals to make himself stand out from the rest of the pack.

Advantages

It's a ludicrously easy industry to enter too – all you need is a computer, Internet access and time. There's plenty of demand for cheap work to get you started, and fair rates for good work if you can do it.

Web design is not without its benefits. Client work is endlessly varied, and you're always learning new things.

Ideal for you, if?

You have technical knowledge and know how to build a website

You love working with computers

You love doing creative things and designing

Other than the above, absolute fundamentals that a web designer should have are:

1. Be familiar with the entire design process: Web design can also overlap with graphic design.

2. Know HTML like the back of your hand: Knowing HTML comes down to coding

3. Understand the finer points of creating a killer copy: As a web designer, you'll be asked to do more than design; you'll sometimes also be asked to create site copy.

4. Commit to constant learning: The phrase "There's always better" is what you should live by as a web designer. One big reason to always be open to learning more is the fact that new trends are always emerging in web design.

5. Develop some business skills: A lot of web designers work freelance at one point or another in their careers, so it only stands to reason that you should develop those all-important business skills. You are your own business, and the highly prized service you are selling is your web design talent.

6. Master the art of great listening: Since you work with clients based on what they tell you they want for their website needs, it only stands to reason that you have to become a master listener.

Strategies to success

Business owners don't value your HTML skills or your time. They value vendors who produce results. Business owners are concerned with what puts money in their pocket or what keeps money in their pocket. If your service doesn't directly impact their bottom line, you're not selling what they're buying.

Writing a proposal is a poor way to close a deal. Offer to write one instead of simply asking for the sale. Learn to close a deal on a verbal agreement, then write the proposal to finalize the sale. So don't write a proposal unless the client has agreed to sign it.

Never Agree to "Final Payment Upon Completion: Obtaining content from the client is one of the most challenging aspects of web design. It may be on dangerous ground when the contract stipulates that the client can make final payment upon completion. Conceivably, a client can delay the project for any number of reasons that are beyond one's control and one can never see that "final payment."

Two Are Better than One: Consider <u>partnerships which might generate more revenue than sole proprietors</u>.

Most web designers constantly work just to keep their clients happy because *unhappy clients don't pay their bills*. Regardless of how good their legal contracts are, a web design company that pisses off their clients won't stay in business for long, and to keep clients happy sometimes means compromising your work to do what you're told.

Web design can make for a satisfying career. But the road isn't easy: You'll need to be able to market your skills effectively to stand out. Network as much as possible. You can start a blog, speak at local events, and learn from others in your field. You'll also need to have the skills to complete complex projects and the personality to please demanding customers.

Disadvantages

But at the lower end of the spectrum, there are many, many companies fighting for the same small amount of work. It's an easy market to enter, but at the same time, it's quite difficult to make a success of things.

Clients were one's bosses, and sometimes one is at the mercy of their whim. Some clients are amazing and wonderful, but there might also be some clients who are misguided, tyrannical and flat-out bonkers too.

www.ingramcontent.com/pod-product-compliance
Lightning Source LLC
Chambersburg PA
CBHW070237190526
45169CB00001B/211